Introduction

Several years ago, in a we[illegible] Thame, we overheard the landlord claiming to have one of the oldest pubs in the town. This assertion led us to ponder the question. *How did he know that?* And more importantly; *Was he correct?*

Some years later, after many hours of detailed research, we had established that the pub in question, the Rising Sun, although occupying one of the oldest buildings in the town was in fact one of the most recent pubs to open, and also that until 1960 it was only licensed to sell beer. This we found to be typical of the way that much of the local historical evidence can be misinterpreted and thus result in the many and varied conflicts of opinion about Thame's history.

It is our hope that in this book we will be able to answer many of the questions that we have been asked about the local pubs, both past and present; whether it is their location, age or their significance to the town.

Before we go further it is important that we should establish a definition for a public house. Tavern, inn, hotel, ale-house, beer-house or public house, each one was different in its own way with clearly defined distinctions between them. However with the passing of the centuries these differences became blurred. Our contemporary hotels may be considered the equivalent of the inn of yesteryear, offering food and accommodation on a considerable scale. The pub or public house is the descendant of the ale-house, smaller than the inn, and until the seventeenth century was legally forbidden to offer lodgings. The urban counterpart of the ale-house was the tavern which tended to serve mainly wine rather than beer. Beer-houses were a follow on from the ale-house as a result of the

1830 Beer Act, and were only allowed to serve beer. Nowadays we find that all these separate licensed establishments are commonly lumped together under the euphemism "pub", and apart from perhaps the modern trend for theme pubs, it is this earlier individuality that has gone on to make the essential elements of the typical English pub. As far as this book is concerned we will adopt the expression that seems to sit most aptly with the property.

The evolution of the inn in Thame undoubtedly started as far back as the thirteenth century, or even earlier. At that time Thame was divided into three distinct administrative areas; Old Thame, New Thame and Priestend, and this segregation remained until the re-organisation of local government in the mid-nineteenth century. Planned market towns were popular developments in medieval times, and the town centre of Thame that we know today is essentially the manor of New Thame that was planned by the Bishop of Lincoln in the twelfth century. A major feature of these planned towns was the opportunity for the townsmen to have tenure of land which previously had only been held by the crown or the church. These thin plots of land lay on either side of the main street and were originally intended to provide for the self sufficiency of a family. These are known as burgage plots from the word "burger" meaning "of the town". The town of New Thame was imposed on the then existing manor of Thame, the remaining parts of which subsequently became known as the manor of Old Thame. Priestend remained as a separate manor in the area to the south of the main Old Thame settlement.

New Thame prospered as a market town and, alongside the markets, inns and ale-houses evolved to serve the traders and visitors from the surrounding area, as well as the local populace. By the eighteenth century the town had developed as far as the limit of the current Upper High Street. In the nineteenth century Thame expanded eastwards beyond the bounds of New Thame towards the railway and into a part of the town that has developed its own architecture. Throughout this development of the town there has

Thame Inns Discovered

Allan Hickman
David Bretherton

First published November 2000 by
Daal Publishing
8 Berkeley Road
Thame OX9 3TQ

Supported by Unique Pub Company, Thame

Designed and set in 12 point Garamond
By Claire Hickman, v2

ISBN No: 0-9539331-0-5

Printed in England by MP Printers, Thame

Front Cover picture *The Rising Sun in the early 1920s, the car is a Singer10 and the man with the apron may well be the licensee Mr Dover.*

Contents

From the towns all Inns have been driven:
From the village most:
Charge your hearts or you will lose your Inns
And you will deserve to have lost them.
But when you have lost your Inns,
Down your empty selves,
For you will have lost the last of England.

Hilaire Belloc
British poet (1870-1953)

Acknowledgements

The authors would like to thank the following for their assistance, without which this book would not have been produced.

Members of Thame Historical Society, Sue Glover at Oxford Magistrates Court; Staff of Oxfordshire Archives, Centre for Oxfordshire Studies and Thame Library. Michael Newitt, Margaret Youens, Derek Brown, Maurice Kirtland and Mrs N.D.Lawrence for the loan of photographs, Mary Hodges and Phil Williams for research assistance, Claire Hickman for the layout of the book; Sue Hickman and Margaret Bretherton for their tolerance and support during the last few years;

Dr Frederick Gymer Parsons D.Sc., F.R.C.S., F.S.A.

Dr Parsons was Professor of Anatomy, University of London and Research Fellow in Anthropology at St Thomas' Hospital where he was for many years a lecturer and demonstrator. He was the author of the history of St Thomas's in three volumes and a contributor of some 30 articles to Encyclopaedia Britannica. In his later life he became an active local historian and published a History of Monks Risborough. He retired to live with his eldest son Henry at the Swan and did much of his writing in an upstairs room overlooking the market. Whilst there he wrote his "Inns of Thame" which was published in the Thame Gazette in 1944 a year after his death.

We are indebted to the research carried out by Dr. Parsons. In the "Inns of Thame" he relies heavily on the research notes of the late Mr Henry Birch (Solicitor) and three rate returns of 1825, 1832 and 1838 for his evidence of dating many nineteenth century pubs. Whilst we are confident of the accuracy of Dr Parsons work we have not been able to verify the detail, for we have been unable trace the research notes or rate returns or indeed Mr Everett who loaned them to Dr Parsons. If any reader should be able to throw light on their whereabouts, then we shall be extremely grateful.

View of the High Street in the early 1900s showing the Nags Head, Black Horse, White Horse. Woods Ale House stood at one time on site of the church

always been a preponderance of pubs in a far higher concentration than the national average per head of population, a fact on which the standard references to the history of Thame all concur. This could have several explanations; perhaps many of them were only small houses run as a sideline by the alewife; maybe they only opened on market days to serve the large number of visitors. Or was it perhaps

Comparative Table of Licences held in Thame (1587 to 1994)

Reference	Year	Licences	Population
Corn Returns	*1587*	*19 "Licensed Vittelers"* *3 "Unlicensed Vittelers"* *1 Common Brewer*	*2000*
Victuallers Recognisances	*1753*	*42 Licensed Victuallers*	*2200*
Trade Directories	*1864*	*18 Innkeepers* *14 Beer Retailers*	*3250*
Brown and Guest	*1906*	*19 Full Licences* *16 Beer-houses* *3 Off licences*	*2911*
Licensing Records	*1910*	*16 Full Licences* *13 Beer-houses*	*3000*
Licensing Records	*1994*	*15 On Licences* *5 Club Licences* *8 Restaurant* *7 Full off-licences*	*10500*

the poor quality of the local water that encouraged the population to quench their thirst with the local brew. The twentieth century saw yet further growth of the town, mainly on the northern and north-eastern fringes. Although this century saw the town almost double in population, the number of pubs significantly decreased. However the number of licensed outlets for the purchase of alcohol remained fairly constant with the opening of bars in various sports and social clubs, together with a large increase in the off licence trade.

Despite this large number of inns we can only deal in this book with those premises for which records provide either a specific name or location. Many other inns are known to have existed, particularly prior to the eighteenth century, but we have not yet been able to establish their identity. Many of the pubs can often only be identified from a single reference in a property deed or rate return, others however occur more frequently in licensing records and trade directories. These, together with many other sources have been researched to provide an extensive record of the pubs in Thame over the past five hundred years, and a list of these source documents is contained in the bibliography.

We have organised the book into a number of chapters which provide a guide around the streets of Thame. Each of the pubs and inns is described separately, with a discussion regarding its location, history and importance within the town. Where appropriate, possible origins to the name of the pub or inn are suggested, although in many instances alternative origins may be equally valid.

The history of the inns of Thame, like those of the rest of the country, has been greatly influenced over the years by national and local government legislation. Rather than disrupt the Thame story with lengthy descriptions of these events, we have provided a more detailed explanation in a separate chapter at the end of the book.

Chapter One

Cornmarket and the South Side of the High Street

A series of ale-houses and inns developed on the south side of the Upper High Street to serve the part of the market that dealt mainly in livestock. Today, only the **Nags Head** remains, but in previous times there were establishments with names such as the **Fox**, the **Angel**, and the **Angel and Crown**.

Modern view of Upper High St, showing No 39 (Angel) No 41 (Fox) and No 44 (Nag's Head)

Behind the eighteenth century facade of what is now a private residence at number 39 Upper High Street stands a much older building of timber frame construction. At one time this was the

Angel Inn and although its earliest known recorded use as an inn was back in 1688, it could possibly date back considerably earlier. In 1820 Thame Charities still listed the **Angel** as yielding six shillings and eight pence (a noble) to the church. It was not uncommon for many of these charitable gifts to have continued for several years after the original legacy had been granted. Since all the known legacies to the church (as opposed to later legacies being given to the parish) date to the sixteenth century, it is likely that the **Angel** can be similarly dated. By 1713 its name had changed to the **Angel and Crown**. For many years the innkeeper was a Leonard Walker who was fined in 1726 at the Oxfordshire Quarter Sessions for keeping an unlicensed ale-house. He died in 1739 and the premises only continued to operate as an inn for about another twenty years.

Number 41 Upper High Street was for many years the **Fox**. In 1838 this was recorded as being the **Old Angel Beer Shop**, and is probably a typical example of a name being taken from the earlier inn in the nearby vicinity. However, by the late 1840s it had changed its name to the **Fox.**

The Fox in 1904 with Alfred and Emily Youens and young son Richard

One of its most notable licensees was Richard Youens who in addition to being a victualler also ran a successful basket making business from the **Fox** for 30 years in the late nineteenth century. He was succeeded by his son Alfred whose untimely death while collecting osiers in Haddenham Low in 1906 left his five year old son to carry on the business. The beer-house only gained a Full Licence when taken over by the Aylesbury Brewery Company in 1971, and twenty years later it became a victim of the restructuring of the pub trade.

It still serves the people of Thame and the market but now as a fish and chip shop.

The Kings Head as drawn by Rev. F.G. Lee in 1880

The **Nag's Head** with its overhanging gables has probably always catered for the market traders since it was built in the sixteenth century. For many years it was known as the **Kings Head**, and was considered one of the most important inns of Thame. It may even have been more extensive than the present building, perhaps extending along as far as the Fox at number 41, but there is currently no definitive evidence to support this theory.

It is a typical example of a timber framed building of the period, pre-fabricated in the Chilterns before being assembled on site. Thame School owned the property until the early 1800's and after a variety of other owners it was sold by Wallingford Brewery to Morrells Brewery in 1930. Today it still serves beer bearing the Morrells name although sadly no longer brewed in Oxfordshire.

As one of the old inns of the town the **Nag's Head** has always supplied a full range of drinks and in 1959 it was granted a Market Licence, which allowed drinks to be served up to 4.30pm, after the then normal closing time of 2pm. The licence for the **Nags Head** was held by the Battin family from 1787 until 1924, which is the longest association of one family with one pub that has been recorded in Thame. The origin behind the name change from the **Kings Head** may well have been to reflect the horse trade in the nearby market. However the contemporary Civil War account published by the Royalist followers, seems more appropriate and would have been enough for any landlord to want to change the name of his inn.

The parliamentary army was in Thame and came across a group of the King's soldiers, one of whom, as an ex-parliamentary soldier, they saw as a traitor. He claimed that he was no traitor but had changed allegiance, because he found he was unable to lift his hand against his lawful sovereign. The King's men were taken prisoner, and the parliamentary soldiers resolved instantly to hang the traitor and they chose the nearest gibbet to hang him from. Unfortunately the sign of the King's Head was already hanging from this frame. He was treated extremely cruelly with taunts and jibes and then just before he died, they turned the man's face towards the sign itself and jeeringly said "Nay sir! you must speak one word with your King before you go, you are blindfold and he cannot see and bye and bye you shall both come down together".

Another aspect of the Nags Head history was its association with the lace ladies of Thame, who in the 19th century would bring their lace and sit on its steps waiting for the merchants from Wycombe and London. They would buy thread from the merchants who in return

The Nags Head in September 1929

would buy their finished lace. Mostly this trade was in pillow lace which local women had made in their cottages all around Thame.

Next door to the Nags Head is the site of the former Wesleyan Chapel but prior to the building of the chapel in 1853 this was for a short period of time Thomas **Wood's Ale-house**.

Moving from the Upper High Street into Cornmarket; at the corner with the narrow Rooks Lane stood the **Fleur de Lys**, which can be traced back to at least 1620. Parsons suggested that the name was taken from the Coat of Arms of the Baldington family. The last known member of the Thame branch of this family married Geoffrey Dormer in the reign of Edward IV, and moved to Place House in Friday (now North) Street in 1490, therefore it is possible an inn has stood on this site since those times.

Matthew Crewes and his brother John leased the ***"Fleur de Luce"*** from the Earl of Abingdon in 1715, together with sixteen acres of land in the common field. They paid a yearly rent at the peculiar rate of *"53s 4d, plus the use of one wagon, four horses and two men for one day's work and also to keep one spaniel, hound or greyhound for the said Earl to use."*

This advertisemet for the Black Horse appeared in the 1935 Town Guide

Although some original parts of the structure may remain, the earlier building was substantially demolished in the 1830's and was rebuilt by the Aylesbury Brewery Company as the **Black Horse**. The name Black Horse is claimed to derive from the famous Lincolnshire horses that were a feature of the October fairs in

Thame, but it is more likely that it was conceived as a foil to the **White Horse** that was next door at the time.

The earliest known references to the **White Horse** date back to the late eighteenth century which possibly support the theory of its name being taken from the white horses which were part of the crest of the House of Hanover. Its proximity to the more prosperous Black Horse may have been partly instrumental in the suppression of its licence in 1908.

Cornmarket with signs of Black Horse Hotel, White Horse and Spread Eagle

Francis Seymour, the landlord at the time, tried to continue trading as a Temperance Hotel, but Thame was evidently no more prepared to take up the temperance call in 1909 than it would be now and it only lasted a year.

A few doors further west stands the imposing Georgian frontage of the **Spread Eagle Hotel**, which was built around 1728 as a private residence for the Stone family. It is reputed that the building was constructed on the site of an earlier inn known as the **Oxford Arms**, and in front of what was at that time the **Crown Inn**. Contrary to some people's belief, the **Spread Eagle** was never a coaching inn, and in fact it was not until after 1833 when the property was bought by Charles Simmonds that the use of the current building changed from a house to a hotel. The enterprising Charles Simmonds later built a brewery in the back garden, and this was probably built on the site of the former **Crown Inn**.

The **Spread Eagle** was, for a number of years, the principle meeting place in the town. Typical groups to utilise its assembly rooms were for instance;

The County Court until the new Court House was built in 1861
A drill room for the Oxfordshire Volunteers in the1860's
A meeting place for the Horticultural Society in 1848
A meeting place to discuss the extension of the railway via Princes Risborough through to Thame in 1857.
The Thursday drill room for a company of the Territorials after their formation in 1909
The Weekly drill room for Special Constables during WW1.
A regular auction room for much of the property around Thame.

By 1922, when John Fothergill bought the **Spread Eagle**, it was already renowned as the social centre of the district under the Lidington family, its owners for many years. The eccentric Fothergill, however, drove out the "farmers and hunting folk" and

The Spread Eagle in the 1920's

attracted his own clientele. Visitors came from far and wide to meet this most individual of innkeepers and partake of his excellent food and hospitality. He kept an unusual record of his more famous clients by measuring their height on a board inside the hotel, many guests also adding appropriate comment. One of Fothergill's most controversial proposals was to erect an enormous signpost on the pavement outside his inn, and although he did get permission from the local council, it was for many years still considered an obstruction.

John Fothergill (in white coat) standing near to his post outside the Spread Eagle

The sign itself was designed and built by a local blacksmith Ralph Timms, but one night during Christmas 1954 it suddenly disappeared. Some say it was "knocked down" by some local soldiers, but this was never confirmed. The current signpost was erected shortly afterwards.

The **Spread Eagle** has been in the charge of the Barrington family since 1949, and today caters for the needs of many of the visitors to the town. Its banqueting suite has for many years provided a location for family and town celebrations.

In addition to his brewery in the back garden of the Spread Eagle Charles Simmonds also opened a drinking house as the **Eagle Tap**. This was on what is still a fine example of one of the burgage plots set out when New Thame was founded in the twelfth century, and which were often bordered by a high stone wall. Much of this wall still exists, skirting what is now Southern Road. The local farm hands would naturally gain access to the beer-house, from the fields, through a gap in the stone wall. Therefore it is likely that this beer-house in the Spread Eagle grounds would later have become known as the **Hole in the Wall**. Bearing in mind its location and secluded access it is not difficult to imagine why the **Hole in the Wall** gained a reputation for becoming a haunt of poachers. Its precise location has not been established, but it is listed in the 1891 census as being accessed from Middle Road. There is still a cottage at the bottom of the Spread Eagle car park and this, as a thatched cottage, was probably the **Hole in the Wall** beer-house.

Documents have recently been discovered that describe a **Greyhound** on the south of the High Street next door to the **Cock** in the early part the eighteenth century. This would place this **Greyhound** on the site of the current **Abingdon Arms** and would probably have occupied the whole frontage of the burgage plot either side of the still existing central archway including what is now Robert Stanley's opticians.

In this series of property deeds the **Greyhound** is said to have once belonged to the Guild of St. Christopher, a guild that was dissolved by Henry VIII during the time of the reformation. It can be conjectured that the name was derived from the heraldic device of Lord Williams that included a greyhound.

The building is much older than its recorded history as a public house, probably dating back to the 1500s, but was badly damaged by fire in 1990 and has been substantially rebuilt.

In the early eighteenth century a notable Thame character made use of the **Greyhound** as his headquarters. James Figg declared himself the

Jimmy Figg of Thame. Champion prize-fighter

champion prize-fighter of England in 1719 and although he fought most of his bouts in Marylebone Park in London he always announced himself as Jimmy Figg of Thame. He is now recognised by most boxing pundits as the first world boxing champion. It is said that there was a portrait of him in the dining room of the **Greyhound** that was highly prized by the landlord Mr Wall. The name of the Inn probably moved across the High Street to the north side in the late eighteenth century.

By 1811 Thomas Clerke had opened a pub called the **Chequers** in the same building in the Cornmarket. The name has heraldic origins but most likely was transferred from the previous **Chequers Alehouse** in the market area. It lasted as the **Chequers** until William Webster took over, and by 1832 had changed its name to the **Abingdon Arms**, probably to honour Montague the 5th Earl of Abingdon, the then owner of large tracts of the land in Thame.

The **Abingdon Arms** has had many owners since then and was one of the few pubs in the area belonging for a time to Hunt

The Greyhound Inn would have occupied the whole of the frontage of this site either side of the central archway

Edmund & Co. of Banbury. It was owned by the chemist Oliver J. Barley for a number of years up until 1948, and in 1982 was displaying the Ushers signboard, a brewery from Trowbridge, Wiltshire. It is today a lively town centre pub serving a wide range of beers and lagers.

A large iron bracket still projects from the wall of number one High Street, now part of Woolworth's store. This supported the sign of the **Fighting Cocks** until 1962. Cock fighting, like in most other parts of the country, was undoubtedly popular in Thame during the eighteenth and nineteenth centuries and there must have once been a cockpit to the rear of this inn during that time. Cock fighting involved specially bred birds equipped with steel spurs and the bouts attracted large sums of money to be wagered on the outcome. The sport had royal admirers in Tudor times but the practice was at one time banned by Oliver Cromwell – it was only finally prohibited by Act of Parliament in 1848.

This area of the Cornmarket must have housed Thame's greatest concentration of public houses in the eighteenth century. Within the confines of the buildings currently occupied by Woolworth's store and immediately to the east of the **Fighting Cocks** was the **Wheatsheaf** and to the east again was the **Windmill**. There was even a **Black Horse** on this site at one time and to add to the confusion the **Wheatsheaf** was previously called the **Cock**.

Continuing along the High Street, immediately to the west of the Fighting Cocks stood the **Red Lion**. The name **Red Lion** is the most common name for an inn in this country, mainly because of the "red lion rampant" of many heraldic devices. This was one of the most important inns in the town during Tudor and Stuart days. It is claimed that King Henry VIII along with Catherine of Aragon and Anne Boleyn (at that time she was a lady-in waiting) were entertained there in 1530. It was from here that the church-wardens regularly bought the communion wine; in 1561 they bought *"15 quarts of Claret and 3 quarts of Malmsey costing 6s 6d at the Lyon"*.

The frontage of the **Red Lion** has changed substantially since it is shown in the background of this picture of the Market Hall depicting life in the sixteenth century and probably occupied the buildings currently housing both Lightfoot's Estate Agency and Martins Newsagents Shop.

16th Century Market House with the sign of the Red Lion on the building to the right

John Harris was licensee up to 1688 and among the property that he left was; "*10 hogsheads of beer in the cellar, valued at £6 and wine and bottles in the wine cellar, valued at £45*". These were incredible sums considering that a good weekly wage at the time was 10d (4p) per day. A hogshead is a cask of beer containing 52 ½ gallons meaning there were 4,200 pints of beer in the cellar of the Red Lion. In those days beer would only have kept for maybe seven days, so it must be considered that the beer was to be consumed in the forthcoming week. That's a lot of drinking considering the size of the population at the time.

One of the most interesting stories about the Red Lion is given in the church-wardens reports of the 1600s, when Thomas Heath was brought before them after he had "*bargained with George Fuller of Chinnor and bought his wife for tuppence for every pound of her weight, which when she was weighed came to 29 shillings and half a farthing*". This made her nearly 13 stone. They spent 2 nights and 2 days in the **Red Lion** during which time "*she was not seen above one hour per day*". He admitted to having sat on the bedside with her and yet he claimed *"not to have carnal knowledge of her body"*, however he was ordered to *"purge himself with six hands"*. Sometime later it was reported that Thomas Heath was her brother and actually bought her out of a bad marriage.

To compensate for the lack of small change in general circulation at this time, local tradesmen issued their own small tokens. The farthing issued by John Harris not surprisingly depicts the **Red Lion**. In the Hearth Tax returns for 1662 he was assessed for 10 hearths, which gives an indication of the size and importance of the inn at that time. The Hearth Tax was an early form of housing rate based on the number of fireplaces in a house. It was very unpopular and only lasted for a few years.

17th Century trade tokens

William Adkins was one of the other inn holders who issued a trade token, but the location of his **Black Lion** remains a mystery. Among the other issuers of trade tokens, who may also have been inn holders, were Dorothy Burgis (The Lion) and Mr John Burges (The Unicorn).

The **Red Lion** had somewhat declined by the time that the diarist Lord Torrington visited Thame in 1785. He described it as *"a bad inn"*, but he was not impressed with Thame in general which he called *"a mean gloomy town"*. Nevertheless the turnpike trustees held their meetings there, and it was the chief posting house and social centre in the early nineteenth century. Having been supplanted by the **Spread Eagle,** it closed in 1847 to make way for a bank.

The next stretch of the High Street is strangely lacking in pubs although it undoubtedly cannot always have been so. An inn that has disappeared from this West Quarter of New Thame is the **Wheele**, given by Margaret Tomlinson to her grandson John in 1623. In 1693 another inn, the **Black Boy** is known to have been somewhere in New Thame with an inn called the **Sword** next door. The name **Black Boy** seems to signify a connection with the crusades, which could equally apply to the **Sword.** The **Wheele** also has religious origins and would have been called the Catherine Wheel prior to the puritan ethos that followed the reformation.

Moving further away from the centre of the market area the **Seven Stars** survived for over 200 years as a combined inn and bakery, but it is suggested by this advertisement from the Thame Gazette of 1886 that the landlords struggled to make it pay. The **Seven Stars** finally closed as a public house in 1898 but now continues its former trade as an eating and drinking house, and is today the Thame Tandoori Restaurant. The Seven Stars, which was a common name throughout the country, may have biblical significance; the Virgin Mary often being depicted in old paintings wearing a seven-starred crown.

TO LET
THE SEVEN STARS INN
THAME
BAKEHOUSE AND GOOD OVEN
ON THE PREMISES
INCOMING LOW; - APPLY
H. PEARCE THE PRESENT TENANT

For a short while after 1838, Mary Arnott ran **Arnotts Beer-house** three doors from Derricks Lane (Southern Road). This was one of the many beer-houses opened as a result of the Beer Act of 1830. This act was designed to encourage beer drinking and suppress the excesses of spirits, particularly gin, by allowing anyone to sell beer on purchase of a licence. The licence was purchased at the local excise office and cost two guineas.

Derricks Lane was probably named after William Derrick victualler at the **One Bell** directly opposite the lane entrance. He had been gradually acquiring the property at the corner of the High Street which, when he died passed on to his son Joseph. When sold to St Clements Brewery in 1861 the property was described as "*...three cottages some years ago converted into one tenement and are now used as a beer-house known by the sign of the Rising Sun ...*"

The **Rising Sun** has prospered on the site since then. It was sold by Halls Brewery (the successors to St Clement's) in 1960 when it was finally granted a full licence to sell wines and spirits as well as beer. It stayed in private hands until recently being bought by Brakspears brewery of Henley.

Lower High Street at the turn of the century showing The Rising Sun. The former Phoenix brewery was in use by Percy Field as a corn warehouse

Much of the appeal of the **Rising Sun** lies in the architecture of the original three cottages that can still be traced both inside and outside the building. The roof gables and overhanging jetty along the

Southern Road aspect add to the attraction of what would seem to be a group of sixteenth century timber frame cottages.

Although a rising sun appears on many families crests dating back to Edward IV and also appears on the badge of the Distillers Company, neither seems appropriate for a beer-house in Thame. More likely the name was chosen to give significance to a new venture in the 1800s.

This is the extent of the southern section of the manor of New Thame; the buildings on the other side of Derricks Lane are in Priestend and those on the opposite side of the High Street, running into Bell Lane are in Old Thame.

Turning to look back up the High Street, the wide market area is dominated by the Victorian Town Hall built in 1889. The northern (left-hand) side of the High Street is the focus of the next chapter.

The High Street looking east before 1887. Note the signboard of the Seven Stars on the right of the picture.

Chapter Two

Buttermarket and the North Side of the High Street

Moving across the road from Southern Road, and going back up towards the town hall, the building half way along the northern side of the High Street, which is now Co-op Travel, occupies the site of what was once the **Crown Inn**. Although this was once one of the five inns at which the church-wardens regularly held their feasts, the other inns being the Bull, the Anchor, the Swan and the Greyhound, little is known of the **Crown.** This is in the main due to it having burned down in 1856, when Joseph Lester was owner and licensee.

Further along the High Street is the building now known as Hampden House. This was during the first half of the nineteenth century the **Greyhound Inn**, but the building was in earlier times the one in which John Hampden is reputed to have died. Educated at Thame School, and later, as MP for Buckinghamshire his refusal to pay "ship-money" was one of the events that led to the start of the Civil War. The fortunes of Thame fluctuated throughout the Civil War, with first Parliament and then the Royalists holding the town. In June 1643 the Parliament forces were challenging Oxford and had established their Headquarters at Thame. At a skirmish with Prince Rupert's army at Chalgrove Field, John Hampden, who was the leader of the local parliamentary army, was wounded. In great pain he returned to Thame and took shelter at the house of Ezekiel Brown which later became the **Greyhound Inn**. Despite the ministrations of King Charles's own physician he died there six days later, on 24th June 1643. His death was a great loss to the parliamentary cause. Quite when the name transferred to this site from the south of the High Street is not known but it probably moved in the late eighteenth century when Richard Wall was landlord.

The Greyhound Inn as drawn by Rev. F.G. Lee in 1846 shortly after it had closed

The early part of the nineteenth century saw the **Greyhound** in use by the church-wardens and between 1823 and 1826 it was here that the Enclosure Commissioners were accommodated. However, possibly due to competition from the Spread Eagle, by 1852 it had closed down and had become a linen and draper's shop.

A few doors up from the **Greyhound**, on the site of what is now Superdrug, once stood the **Sun Inn**. It is in the yard behind the **Sun Inn** that a meeting house was formed for the Presbyterians in 1728, and continued in use, later as a Wesleyan chapel and then as a Baptist chapel, up to the middle of the nineteenth century.

At number 2 Buttermarket was the inn known by the sign of the **Bull**. A prominent inn for many years the **Bull** dates back beyond 1650 when it was left in the will of Stephen Cousin to his daughter Elizabeth Brookes. The building follows the classic sixteenth century timber framed lines and would originally have had over-sailing jetties with a carriageway access through to the rear.

This entrance-way is now the door to what was until recently Taurus china shop. Parsons refers to old inhabitants of Thame remembering farmers' wives sitting in the porch, leading into the yard, with their baskets of butter and eggs for sale. Presumably this was whilst the farmers conducted their business inside.

The Bull when John Fowler was licensee

Probably known at one time as the **Black Bull**, the name may have been taken from a heraldic device but most likely it derives from the Tudor days when the bull's head was the sign used by Henry VIII. The **Bull Inn** was repressed in 1913 on the grounds of frequent changes of licensees and afterwards served for many years as Mundays wines and spirits shop. It was a mere co-incidence that in more recent times china has been sold at the **Bull**. The use of the name Taurus was a further lucky accident, as the owners transferred the name from a previous business.

It is possible that an inn or ale-house stood next to the **Bull** at number 3 Buttermarket. In the title deeds of the property relating to 1792, it is referred to by the name the **Elephant**. At that time, a Mr James Berry held the house as a draper but no further information is available.

Situated in the High Street, next door to the Old Market House, Thomas Edden ran a beer-shop that in 1838 was rated at £10.

However no other record of **Edden's Beer-shop** has been found.

The seventeenth century gabled exterior of the **Saracen's Head** hides a timber framed building that dates back to the fourteenth century. Recent work carried out at the premises, when converting it to the current estate agents office, established the likely felling date of the main timbers as being about 1315.

The building is reputed to have had a vaulted medieval cellar that may have dated back even further. Lupton, in his History of Thame, suggests the brewers who owned the house, removed the vaulting before 1860 in order to gain more room for their casks. He also points out that the house, close by, at the corner of North Street also showed a gothic arch in its cellar. This co-incidence led him to suggest that the three houses from North Street to the **Saracen's Head** stood on the large vaulted basement of an important building which he thought might have belonged to some religious order. Lee, however, has pointed out that a Saracen's head was the crest of the Oxfordshire branch of the Marmion family, who lived in Thame

Buttermarket in 1908 with the sign of the Saracens Head and the empty bracket of the Bull behind.

until the fifteenth century. Although the site of their home is not known he advances that their mansion covered these groined cellars on the north side of the Butter Market and that later the **Saracen's Head** inn was built on part of its site and adopted the Marmion crest as its sign.

The Saracens Head in the mid 1980s

The accounts for Thame School in 1575 give the tenant as one Richard Pitman paying a rent of 26s 8d per half year to New College Oxford. Thame School continued to own the premises until 1877 when it was sold along with other property and bought by the then licensee Francis Seymour. Halls Brewery purchased it in 1913 and it finally stopped selling beer in 1992. In the early twentieth century the **Saracen's Head** gained a reputation as a centre for the sporting fraternity and was at one time the headquarters of Thame Football Club.

Moving from the confines of the Buttermarket into the open space of the Upper High Street, the building that immediately demands attention is the Swan. However four doors west of the Swan, John King owned and ran a beer-house in the 1830s. This doubled as a baker's shop and went under the name of **King's Ale-house**. This sign probably hung from the iron bracket which now projects from the roof of the Prince of India restaurant.

The **Swan** has been a prominent inn in Thame since Sir John Clerke built it in the early part of the sixteenth century. The Clerke family crest is of three swans and it is from this that the **Swan** inn most likely takes its name. The eighteenth century front hides the much earlier timber framed building that originally had two over-sailing jetties to the front. Until fairly recent times there was stabling for thirty to forty horses at the rear stretching back to Wellington Street. It was not however a true coaching inn, but one of the venues in Thame from which coaches would leave for other local towns on the main coaching routes; typically to Aylesbury, and even Tetsworth, where the Swan's namesake was a main coaching inn. During these times a glass roof covered the first or inner yard to provide protection for the visitors.

The **Swan** was a popular eating place for the church-wardens with many references in their accounts going back to 1634. This popularity continued into the 1930s where in the large old-fashioned kitchen a farmers' ordinary was provided on market days for two shillings and the bar was used by farmers for settling their market transactions. An "ordinary" was a set meal served communally around a large table.

Originally part of the Earl of Abingdon's estates, Hannah Bennet a wealthy widow bought the property in 1769 and held it until 1790. The **Swan** remained in private hands until the bankruptcy of another widow, Hannah Phillips in 1832, when it was repossessed by William Hall of Oxford. It thus came into the hands of Halls Brewery and remained with them until they closed the **Swan** in the late 1970s. In 1985 the whole burgage plot at the rear was redeveloped into what is now Swan Walk, and the **Swan** itself re-opened.

The Swan when George Baker was landlord

The Stone family records contain details of an inn called the **George** that existed in New Thame from 1769 to at least 1785. Although the exact location of the **George** is uncertain, the property deeds show that it was eventually sold in 1842 to John Scadding, who was a schoolmaster, along with "*a garden now used as a playground*". Census records indicate that this was likely to be in the Upper High Street at number 27 and 27a and was part of a mansion house that at one time stood on the site. Although the name **George** is often used to honour the patron saint of England, it is usually coupled with a dragon. In this instance it is more likely that the name is in honour of the king of England, and the absence of a number suggests an association with George I (1714-1727).

Also in this area between 1750 and 1762 was an inn known as the **Three Pigeons**. During this period it was run by Elizabeth Dobbinson but shortly afterwards it was sold to become a private residence.

The Pearce memorial gardens are built on what was once White Hound Pond, where animals would have been watered prior to entering the market. In 1864 Mr Henry Birch wrote that the **White Hound Inn** once stood opposite White Hound pond, and that it had burned down probably 200 years earlier. At that time this would have been the eastern extent of New Thame and the field beyond the boundary (and thus in Old Thame) was known as White Hound Close. If an old inn did exist in this part of town, it is likely that it was called the **White Hound.**

Chapter Three
Middle Row

The original cigar shaped market place planned towards the end of the twelfth century by the Bishop of Lincoln had few permanent buildings obstructing the central area. However, in-fill started to take place during the thirteenth century, this area eventually becoming known as Middle Row.

One of the first buildings to be erected would have been a building used to control and administer the market, and the site on which the **Bird Cage** now stands would in all probability have been this first market house. It is centrally positioned within the confines of the High Street and, as the only permanent building, would have commanded a dominant position over the market, facing as it does down the High Street. It should be noted the view of the **Bird Cage** from the Cornmarket that we enjoy today is actually the side of the

In this sketch of the Birdcage from the 19th Century the three stages of building are apparent.

The Birdcage in the days of Watlington Brewery ownership. Henry Summersby was the landlord. Note the blacked-in oriel windows and lack of access from the shambles

building. The true front is facing into the Shambles and if it were not for the large building of the Nat West Bank then it would command a good view down the High Street.

The earliest parts of the current building date from the late thirteenth century, and the building was constructed in phases over the next 100 years, the central two-storey section being the oldest part. The later, but more prominent, part has many impressive features; massive elm corner post timbers; three storeys over-sailing on three sides with the hugely impressive dragon beams and two oriel windows with fine wooden tracery work. All of these would have indicated a building of great importance to the inhabitants of fourteenth century Thame. In keeping with other market houses of this time, the lower storey would have been open for use by the market traders. Later maybe, bars could have been inserted to keep out undesirables.

The cellar with its moulded stone doorway and aumbries (wall recesses for religious vessels) may be part of the original thirteenth century market hall, for it had a separate entrance direct from the street, evidence of which still remains today. This may suggest some early ecclesiastical use, but more likely an area for storage of parish arms and armour, or even perhaps an early prison associated with the local Bishop's court which would probably have been held in the market hall above.

The earliest date the building was used as an inn cannot be certain, but it would have been sometime after the erection of the new market hall, on the site of the current town hall, during the fifteenth century. In 1529 *a tenement called the Cage* was the property of the Guild of St Christopher, a local merchants' guild founded by Richard Quartermain in 1447. The **Cage** was then granted, by Edward VI, to Sir John Williams who rented it to James Roose for eight shillings a year. Around 1600, the property, like much of Thame, belonged to Lord Bertie (Earl of Abingdon) and was held as copyhold by a yeoman Philip Bird. Could this be when it became **Bird's Cage**? Nevertheless it continued in legal documents to be referred to as "*a tenement named the Cage*" up to the 1780s. Edward Turner was the first licensee to formally use the name **Bird Cage** in 1787. One of his successors as licensee was Ann Turner who used the name **Bird in the Cage** from 1821 to 1847.

During the Napoleonic Wars most English towns were required to accommodate French prisoners of war and the larger houses with cellars or attics proved ideal locations. It would therefore have been Edward Turner who entertained sixteen Napoleonic prisoners in his cellar from 1805. The current landlord discovered a ball and chain of the period during the recent re-decoration.

No account of the **Bird Cage** would be complete without a mention for the ghost of the Restless Soul. One time landlady Pat Ellis who claimed to have encountered the Restless Soul in the top storey of the pub believed it to be that of a leper who had been stoned to death by the people of Thame.

Right: The Birdcage as it appears today

The **Bird Cage** was bought by Simmonds Brewery of Reading when it was put up for sale by Watlington Breweries in 1906. The licensee at the time of the sale, Charles Blood, went on to become Mayor of Thame in the 1920s. The early picture shows the building complete with stucco render that Maurice Howe, the then estates manager for Simmonds Brewery, ordered to be removed in 1948. (Would this have been allowed today?). Ownership was transferred to Courage in 1963 and the recent changes in the way England's pubs are controlled and managed sees the **Bird Cage** now owned by the Unique Pub Co. who have their headquarters at Mill House on the outskirts of Thame.

The Anchor as a Commercial Inn prior to 1906. The gent in the bowler hat is Robert Guntrip drayman for Aylesbury Brewery Co. (He was also licensee at the Woolpack)

Another of the prominent inns in the eighteenth and nineteenth centuries was the **Anchor,** which was located at the west end of Middle Row, now Simmonds and Lawrence Estate agents. This building is one of a pair of timber framed market stalls that were erected in front of the Market Hall (Bird Cage), the other one being what is now Donald Butler's furniture shop. The building was originally two storeys of close boarded construction with over-sailing jetties on three sides. Many of the interior timbers are now exposed but due to fire in the 1980s little of the roof structure remains. The construction of the lower floor does however indicate a building dating back to the sixteenth century.

The **Anchor** sign hung from the bracket now supporting the Witch Ball. For many years, one of the inns used by the church wardens for their annual feasts, its trade must have been flagging by the early part of the nineteenth century. Its attempted resurgence as a commercial hotel obviously proved unsuccessful and Aylesbury Brewery Company closed the inn in 1921 just 10 years after they had acquired it.

On the opposite corner of the block of Middle Row stands a pub

Oxford Arms prior to 1906 when James Gibbs was landlord.

now called the **Market Square,** which for many years was known as the **Oxford Arms.** The current mock-Tudor building was built about 1930 and replaced an older ale-house that had existed on the site since at least the early eighteenth century. This earlier inn had supplanted an Oxford Arms that had formerly stood on the site of the Spread Eagle.

The earliest known licensee was Robert Howland, a carrier, who at the Quarter Sessions of Easter 1757 claimed "*to have missed hay and wood out of his yard at the Oxford Arms*". Richard Goodgame confessed to the crime and was fined £40.

Although originally an ale-house it was only in the 1930s when the current building was erected by Wethereds Brewery that the **Oxford Arms** was granted its full drinks licence.

The only other building known to have served alcohol on the plots of Middle Row was the **Bull Ale-house.** This small ale-house, owned by John Coles in 1838, was probably at the extreme eastern end of Middle Row, possibly where the betting shop now is. There does not seem to be any connection with the **Bull Inn** and the ale-house likely took its name to attract farmers and butchers from the cattle market over the road.

Although not strictly in Middle Row, the only building to invade the open space of the upper market area was built as an ale-house in the eighteenth century. Now the Tourist Information Office the **Chequer Ale-house** is described in sale documents of 1786 as "*all that tenement in Hoggsherd Hill being then the Chequer ale-house with forge attached*". This is a typical example of running an ale-house as a sideline to another trade, in this case a smithy.

Hoggsherds Hill describes the rise at the top of North Street, an area where the pig market was located prior to its removal to the Hog Fair at the end of Brook Lane. At the sale the building was

Upper High Street in 1880 showing the Oxford Arms and Market House (formerly Chequer Ale-house)

bought by public subscription to be converted to a meeting house and chapel for the Countess of Huntington's Connection, which was a little known branch of the Congregationalist church and it remained in this use until 1833.

Chapter Four
Friday Street and Old Thame

Moving away from the area of the main town centre and into North Street, this was for several centuries known as Friday Street until the change to its current name in 1874. It is believed the name originated from the fish market that was held in the street every Friday and which was located en-route to the town fish ponds (now under some of the modern houses of Lea Park).

Invariably, this market association resulted in the existence of many drinking establishments. In the eighteenth and early nineteenth centuries there must have been many inns and ale-houses competing for the custom of the local market, but evidence of only one, the **Blue Man**, can be directly linked back to those times.

The building at the top of Friday Street, on the corner with Upper High Street, served as Parrott's ale and wine store during the latter part of the nineteenth century. Some years earlier, in the yard at the rear, stood one of Thame's three breweries. This was started by Edmund Seamons but for most of its time was operated by Joseph Child Tingle.

The Wheatsheaf in the 1950s

A little further down, what is now the Cancer Research shop was at one time the **Wheatsheaf**. First recorded as a beer-house in 1842 and probably serving beer from the brewery next door, it may have taken its name to tempt some of the corn merchants away from the High Street. However its first licensee, A

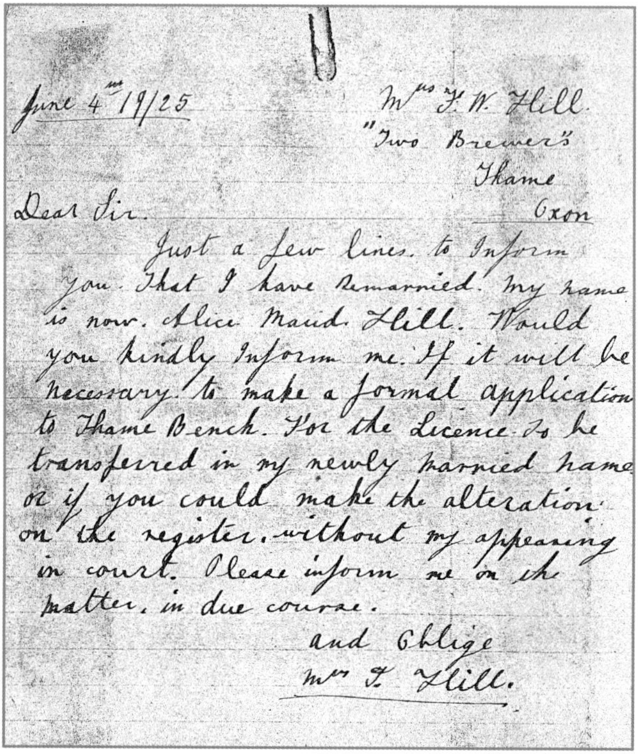

June 4th 19/25

Mrs F. W. Hill.
"Two Brewers"
Thame
Oxon

Dear Sir.

Just a few lines. to Inform you. That I have remarried. my name is now. Alice Maud. Hill. Would you kindly Inform me. If it will be necessary. to make a formal application to Thame Bench. For the Licence to be transferred in my newly married name or if you could make the alteration on the register. without my appearing in court. Please inform me on the matter. in due course.

and Oblige
Mrs F. Hill.

The Letter from Alice Hill in 1925

William Howland, was in fact a cattle dealer. The pub only ever held a beer licence and in 1956 when it was sold by Halls Brewery this was not renewed by the new owners.

On the corner of North Street and Wellington Street stands the **Two Brewers.** Although the building is of some considerable age, like the **Wheatsheaf**, its life as a public house can only be traced to its beginning as a beer-house in 1832. At one time owned by the W.G. Weller Brewery of Amersham, and then Benskins of Hertfordshire, it was only allowed to serve beer up until 1961, when it was finally granted a full wines and spirit licence. A letter from Alice Hill dated 1925 gives an indication of how the licensees were respectful to the Licensing Bench in those times. Two years later, however Alice was fined £3 for serving beer out of hours and shortly afterwards lost her license. Now in the hands of Greene

King, it provides sustenance for the local inhabitants as well as to people attending the nearby cattle market.

> LOT 22.
>
> **The "BRITANNIA" Beer House,**
>
> **THAME.**
>
> At the corner of Wellington Street and North Street.
>
> A stucco and tiled Property.
>
> CONTAINING:
>
> Tile-paved Tap Room and Smoke Room, Kitchen, paved Cellar under, Sitting Room and Four Bedrooms.
>
> Large Kitchen Garden in rear.
>
> ALSO
>
> Two Cottages of Five and Three Rooms respectively.
>
> Let to Mr. J. Pember.
>
> FREEHOLD
>
> Subject to a right of Way. Land Tax £1 2s. 9d.

Extract from Watlington brewery sale catalogue 29 December 1906

For many of its early years Charles and Priscilla Bonner ran the **Two Brewers**. The Bonner family were reasonably successful trades' people in Thame during the middle of the nineteenth century, and in 1847 Thomas and Biddy Bonner set up in the **Britannia** just across the road from the **Two Brewers**. By the mid 1880s the pub was owned by Wethereds of Marlow, but it was put up for sale by Watlington Brewery in 1913 when its licence was refused. The building that was the **Britannia** is now known as number 47 North Street, although the address has often changed and over the years it has been variably listed as in Friday Street or in Pound Lane or in Pound Street. Pound Lane, so named because it led to the town animal pound, was renamed Wellington Street by the Victorians. Along Wellington Street the original building on the site of number 54 had been the town bridewell, or house of correction and was developed into the first workhouse of Thame. With the building of the new workhouse on the Oxford Road, it became a lodging house and then a beer-house. The pub was initially known as the **Sailor's Return**, before gaining its more popular name of the **Jolly Sailor** in the 1850's.

Three former inns/pubs as they appear today. l-r Half Moon, Blue Man, Jolly Sailor

The old timber structure was completely gutted by fire in 1905, after which the current building was erected. The beer-house gained its full licence in 1949 when owned by The Aylesbury Brewery Company. It endured a certain reputation during the 1970's and 1980's, centring around one of its more regular customers, the comedian Larry Grayson. It was a reputation which, in 1985, its new tenant wished to shed and he changed the name to the **Wellington Hotel**. Despite being purchased by the brewers Fuller, Smith and Turner in 1988 it was never able to regain its previous popularity and it finally closed in February 1994.

Across the street from the **Jolly Sailor**, there are a pair of cottages with long front gardens. The right hand of these (now number 7 Wellington Street) was until 1923 the **Half Moon** beer-house. The owner and licensee from 1887 to 1920, James Soanes, was depicted on a painting by Stanley Anderson carrying out his other trade of hurdle making. This painting was exhibited at the Royal Academy in the1930's and it would be of great interest to establish its current whereabouts.

The **Half Moon** is reputed to have been a popular rendezvous for poachers and it is further claimed that these poachers were to blame for many of the scuffles that took place at the pub. It is likely that this was a prime cause in the suppression of this beer-house in the purge of drinking establishment that followed the Great War.

Moving back into Old Thame and North Street, towards the rear entrance to the Waitrose car park, there is a building that was one of the old inns of Thame, the **Blue Man**. The origin of the name is not known but it is rare as an English pub name the only other example being in Grantham. Is this a further example of Thame's early connection with the Diocese of Lincoln? The building is a quaint mix of gables and chimneys and externally is substantially the same today as it may always have been. For many years the **Blue Man** was owned by the Church Commissioners having been left to them in the will of Richard Leaver, in 1723, "*to provide gowns for two poor men and women.*" The **Blue Man** became a victim of the 1904 Licensing Act being the first pub in Thame to be closed after the introduction of the act.

The **Greyhound** across the road, at the corner of Moorend Lane was created by converting two cottages, now numbers 44 and 45 North Street. The name **Greyhound** was introduced here soon after the old Greyhound closed in the High Street. The picture on page 48 shows that it is now structurally much the same as it was when it served beer. Welch Ale Brewery bought the beer-house in 1911 and it survived until 1921 when trade must have been very poor as the licence was approved by the authorities but not taken up.

Greyhound Beerhouse in early 1900s (note mis-use of the word inn)
- A Parsons Entire was a type of beer

The inns in Old Thame would have provided much needed sustenance and rest for the drovers and farmers who were travelling to and from the markets of New Thame. This would have been particularly true for the **Red Cow**. Situated on the Aylesbury Road, in the area known for many years as Lashlake, this inn existed on the site next to the Thame Mill before 1750. It would have provided an ideal rest point for travellers on their way to and from the town until better roads and mechanised transport made this unnecessary and the inn became redundant in 1917.

Painting of Red Cow with Thame Mill in background

The picture shows the **Red Cow** with Thame Mill in the background, at that time the mill was owned by Mr Henry

The Red Cow in 1909 when Lewis Baldwin was licensee

Boddington. It was painted just prior to him venturing north to found the well known Boddingtons Brewery in Manchester.

In the middle of the eighteenth century, there were six licensed premises in Old Thame. The **Red Cow** and **Blue Man** have been mentioned earlier and two others are only known from the names of their licensees. The final two were the **One Bell** and the **Four Horseshoes**.

The **One Bell Inn** gave its name to One Bell Lane and which is now known simply as Bell Lane. The **Bell Inn** itself probably gained the name the **One Bell** to distinguish it from the **Six Bells**. Situated at number 80 High Street what is now the shop of P&D House, its licence in 1753 was held by John Eustace. This was taken over in the 1770's by William Derrick, who later gave his name to Derricks Lane (now Southern Road). Before the coming of the railway to Thame in 1862 a coach ran from here each morning to Aylesbury Station for travellers to London and returned in the evening. The inn closed in October 1914 in strange circumstances, as the letter from Sgt Harris illustrates. After the closure Henry Reynolds offered the use of the **One Bell** for Belgian Refugees and then early in 1919, he gave it for use as a club-house for the

The Bell in the early 1900s

"Comrades of the Great War" which at that time had 600 members in Thame. Captain Terrell MP opened the club in March 1921 and it survived as a club for many years, and finally as a Labour and Social Club, before closing in the mid 1970s.

The **Four Horseshoes**, despite its location at the far end of Park Street, was still part of the manor of Old Thame and existed from the early 1700s, long before this part of the town was built up. Lupton in his History of Thame refers to there being a Three Horseshoes in Park Street as well as the Four Horseshoes. However there is no other evidence to support this and it is most likely to be caused by early references to this pub as the Three Horseshoes or just the Horseshoes.

Like the other inns of Old Thame the **Four Horseshoes** would have provided rest for travellers to and from the markets of New Thame, in this case from the direction of the Chilterns and areas to the east. The inn owed much to its success in the late nineteenth century to the coming of the railway with a new lease of life serving travellers of a different era. At one stage its name was changed to

OXFORDSHIRE CONSTABULARY.

Thame Station, Oct 1st. 1914.

re/ One Bell, fully Licensed
Lower High Street Thame,
Hall & Co. Oxford (Brewers,

Sir

I respectfully beg to report for your information, that the above named premises was up till Tues. last 29th ultimo, in the occupation of Thomas Cast, who left & handed over the keys to Mr. Hinton of Hall's Stores Thame,

These premises were leased from Mr. Henry Reynolds, of Notley Abbey Bucks, & the lease expired at 12 Oct on Tues 29th Septr. & the keys has been handed over to Mr. Reynolds, so now the house is closed,

I am Sir

Your Obt Servant
A. J. Harris.
Sergt

Mr. G. Sarrell
Supt & Deputy C.C.
Oxford

The Letter from Sergeant Harris

reflect its new clients and it became the **Four Horseshoes Railway Hotel** or sometimes just the **Railway Commercial Hotel**. The property outlived the railway but in 1996 surrendered to the growing trend of public houses becoming residential properties, although the planning authorities refused permission to demolish the building altogether. Despite this new development the bounds of the original farm that in 1788 Thomas Burnard bought at auction for £151, are still traceable today. It was the enterprising landlord John Young who set up the motor garage next door in 1903 complete with a skilled mechanic on the premises.

The Four Horseshoes Railway Hotel sometime before Watlington Brewery sold out in 1906

Chapter Five
Priestend

The manor of Priestend occupied the area to the south of the Lower High Street and to the west of New Thame. It included the road out of town that we now know as Priestend.

Mid eighteenth century records show victuallers at three premises in Priestend yet of these only the **Six Bells** can be named today. The **Six Bells** is a timber-framed building of the sixteenth century. Almost certainly it was prefabricated of oak in the Chilterns and then re-assembled on site. Evidence of the over-sailing jetty to the front can clearly be seen in the ceiling timbers of the bars and in the inner doorframe at the entrance to the snug bar. One unusual feature of the Six Bells is the position of its cellar, with its original sixteenth century door, in the centre of the building and accessed through a public area. This indicates that the building was once much smaller than it is now, and indeed, the confines of the original building can still be traced through the large chamfered beams in the main bar.

The Six Bells in the 1890s. The cottage on the left was incorporated into the inn in 1938

The name **Six Bells** undoubtedly stems from its proximity to the church, but there have been eight bells hanging in the belfry for many years. The first mention of six bells is in 1545 but these were re-cast to eight bells in 1664, a moment commemorated in their casting in the poem below.

I AS TREBL BE GIN
Six hundred-weight

I AS SECOND SING
Seven hundred-weight

I AS THIRD WILL RING
Eight hundred-weight

I AS FORTH IN MY PLACES
Ten hundred-weight

I AS FIFT WILL SOUND
Twelve hundred-weight

RICHARD KEENE CAST ME 1664
Seventeen and a half hundred-weight

Inscriptions cast into the six Church Bells

The first recorded use of the name **Six Bells** for the inn was almost a hundred years later when Grace Gibbons was licensee. On 23 January 1772 the church-wardens were billed for food and drink at the **Six Bells**;

For one quart of Beer	*total 1s 4d*
For 2 Quarts at 8s	*total 4s 0d*

Further evidence of the cost of food in the eighteenth century came to light during alterations to the building in 1938 with the discovery of scraps of receipts for meat and cheese purchased by the landlord Richard Gibbons. Copies of these various receipts now hang in the bar. These alterations enlarged the pub by combining a passageway and the cottage next door into a new lounge, and also replaced the old fireplace and chimney with the new bar.

Halls' Oxford Brewery owned the pub from 1911 until selling it to

The Crown with Thomas Grant and family at the turn of the century.

Fullers in 1988. Fullers have tastefully redesigned and decorated the building and it now makes a pleasant respite from the bustle of the town centre. There is a large beer garden that can be very crowded with students in term time.

At the corner of the High Street and Priestend was the **Crown** beer-house. This was opened by Joseph Lester shortly after his previous pub in the town centre, also called the **Crown,** had burned down in 1856. The **Crown** was de-licensed in 1908, but the building still retains a sign outside announcing this to be "The Old Crown".

Before the building became the **Crown** it was operated for a number of years by Thomas Steeden as the **Black Horse** ale-house. This confusingly was at the same time as the more familiar **Black Horse** hotel was opened in the High Street and may be the reason for the name change to the **Crown**.

Around the corner in Priestend, John and Hannah Price opened the **Plough** Beer-house in the 1830's. Its proximity to the newly constructed workhouse could not have been a co-incidence and

The Plough in Priestend as it appears today

much of its custom would have been from the construction workers. Thomas Blood the licensee in 1891 was described as a beer retailer & agent for Morrells Brewery, although Halls owned the beer-house from 1911 to its closure in 1917.

The census returns of 1871 give Thomas Clifford a licensed victualler as resident in Crendon Road together with his wife, three daughters, a son and two servants. There are very few properties on the Crendon Road and none have any reference to being a pub neither is there any other reference to where this licensed victualler practised.

William Taplin ran a business in the Lower High Street known by the name of **Taplin's Inn**. This was probably the same William Taplin who ran a coach business between Thame and High Wycombe, deciding to provide some profitable refreshment for his fare-paying customers. Like a great number of these beer-houses however, this only survived for a short while in the 1830s.

Chapter Six
Victorian Expansion

The first half of the nineteenth century saw large development mainly towards the east of the town. When the railway came in the 1860s it provided more impetus to the building and the expansion. Of course these new inhabitants would need new drinking houses and the victuallers of Thame did not disappoint them.

The **Star and Garter** beer-house was first recorded in 1861 and described as being in Risborough Road. It was in turn listed as, Towersey Road, Tythrop Terrace, Pound Street and Pound Lane, prior to settling to the current address in Wellington Street at the

Views of the Star and Garter in the nineteenth century

turn of the century. The name was derived from the Most Noble Order of the Garter of which the Star forms part of the insignia and the use of the name celebrated allegiance to Queen Victoria who was head of the order.

Twentieth Century Star & Garter

At the sale of the Watlington Brewery estate in 1906 the **Star and Garter** was bought by Morland Brewery of Abingdon and has served their beers since, although now in association with Greene King. The Wells family ran it as a beer-house from 1881 to 1953 and it only obtained a full licence when Hubert Brown took over the premises.

The building was subject to a major investment by the brewery in 1985 and was substantially rebuilt. It now caters for the local people and visitors alike in the happy atmosphere of a local pub and the only pub in town where the locals can enjoy participating in the local Oxfordshire game of Aunt Sally.

The entrance to Park Street is dominated by the facade of the **Cross Keys.** The **Cross Keys** has imposed itself on the junction since New Road (now East Street) was built in the 1840s with Thomas Burnard as its first licensee.

LOT 23

The "STAR AND GARTER" Beer House,

THAME.

A double-fronted well situated corner Property on the Towersey Road.

CONTAINING:

Parlour, Tap Room, Kitchen, Upland Cellar and Four Bedrooms.

ALSO

Cottage of Four Rooms.

Brick-built and tiled Stabling for Eight Horses, Coach House and Tiled Cart Shed, with Entrance Gates from Road.

Let to Mr. John Wells.

FREEHOLD (Land Tax 14/4).

Extract from Watlington Breaery sale catalogue of 29 December 1906

The name can be associated with Christian heraldry, being a papal symbol. This is not the first use of the name in Thame; in the seventeenth century **Red Lion Inn** the rooms were similarly named, amongst them being one called the Cross Keys in which were twelve leather chairs and twelve tables.

Welch Ale from Chelsea was served up to 1921 when the more local Aylesbury Brewery Company acquired the property. The aptly named Tipple family arrived soon after and stayed until 1956.

The Cross Keys from a postcard of 1908

In the nineteenth century it was a popular practice to re-use the name of a defunct pub when naming a new drinking establishment. This was so when the **Red Lion** beer-house opened in the 1860s. The stone fronted building still stands at 33 Park Street. The stone used is very similar to much of the property built in this area of the town following the development of Park Street and New Road. The **Red Lion** was owned by Wroughton & Threlfall in the late nineteenth century and closed in 1915 soon after being taken over by the Aylesbury Brewery Company.

A pair of small cottages at 41 Park Street was for sixty years the site of the **Woolpack** beer-house. The name harks back to a major trade in Thame's history and may reflect a mini-revival of the wool trade at this time or maybe just reminiscences of an early licensee. A woolpack was a large pack or bale of wool, weighing 240 pounds, prepared for carriage and sale. The **Woolpack** closed in 1908 presumably the subject of suppression by the magistrates.

During this Victorian expansion, Park Street was known as Brick Kiln Lane and much of the property in this area is built of the local brick. A brick-kiln was located on the site of what is today's petrol station. The **Bricklayers Arms** once stood in Brick Kiln Lane and would have been named to attract the men building the houses. The intriguingly named **King of Prussia** also stood in this area sometime in the 1830s. The sign is generally accepted to be named after Frederick the Great who was a great ally of England in the war against the French.

One of the last public houses to be opened in Thame was the **Wenman Arms** at 67 Park Street. It was built on land previously owned by Baroness Wenman of Thame Park who had been

A trio of closed beer-houses, l - r: Red Lion, Woolpack, Wenman Arms

accorded the title by William IV some years earlier. First recorded in 1874 the beer-house had a large number of licensees during its life prior to closure in 1957.

The Wenman Arms in the 1950's

The **Wenman Arms** is still fondly remembered by some of the local inhabitants, one of whom relates a story told by his father:

> *"Between the wars the Wenman was a frequent haunt of the local constabulary, who turned a blind eye to the after-hours drinking. However, after a falling out, the Police raided the Wenman one night, causing confusion by knocking on all the doors together. Not knowing which one to answer, those inside deliberately chose not to open any of them. Eventually the officers did gain entry but by that time could not find anyone still drinking. And so, not to be out done, they booked the landlord for having a dog without a licence."*

The **Wenman Arms** would have shared the custom from the nearby Police Station with the **Falcon Inn**. The **Falcon** opened in 1861 at the same time that the railway came to Thame and was often referred to as the **Falcon Railway Hotel**. In 1900 it was substantially damaged by fire and was rebuilt much as it appears today. The sign of the Falcon possibly relates to the crest of the Dormer family at one time large landowners in Thame. Through the years the **Falcon** has served a variety of different brews; Wheelers Brewery of Wycombe up to 1930, Ashby Staines Brewery from Middlesex in 1931, Simmonds Brewery of Reading up to 1944,

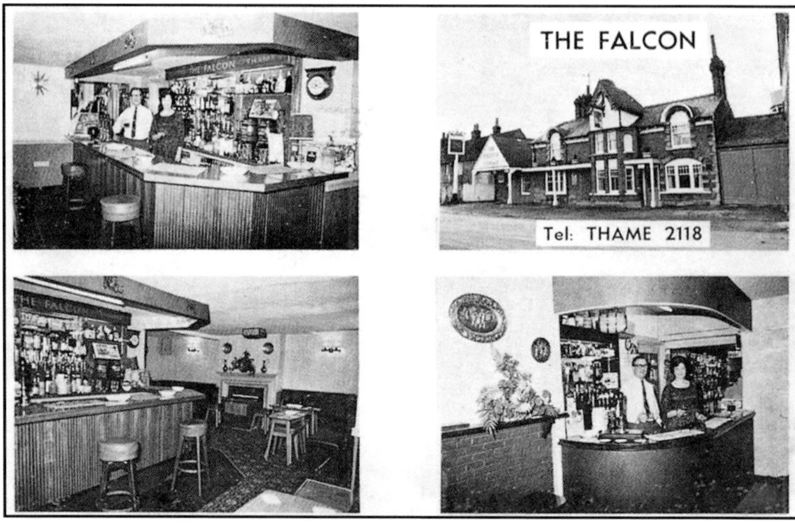

1969 advertising card from hosts Norah and George Bish

Wheelers again up to 1950, then Simmonds again. Courage took it over in 1963 and since 1991 Morlands beer has been sold but now under the guise of Greene King. Despite being named a hotel, only beer could be served, and it was not until George Cole took over in February 1972 that the beer licence was converted to allow wines and spirits also to be sold.

The **Falcon** is the sole survivor of the many drinking establishments of Park Street and today provides a vital service to this part of the town.

Chapter Seven
The Licensees

We have compiled these lists of licensees from the information contained in the various reference documents. Some of the people are referred to as the occupant or tenant but most are known as victualler, beer-seller or innkeeper. Unfortunately the lists are only as complete as the source material will permit and we have not made any attempt to fill in the many gaps. In the reference documents there are numerous additional names of victuallers and beer-sellers that we have not been able to ascribe to a particular pub. Hopefully, as more research is carried out and more material becomes available, we will eventually be able to complete much of the missing information. The earliest reference for many of the pubs does not contain a name for the occupant; in these events we have included the reference date together with "unknown" for the licensee. In the later years joint licensees are recorded and here the names of each of the joint licence holders are included in alphabetical order.

Abingdon Arms

	Chequers
1811 - 1823	Thomas Clerke
1825 -	Thomas Stone
	Abingdon Arms
1830 -	William Webster
1841 -	John Bonner
1842 - 1847	James Price
1850 - 1898	Jacob Watson
1899 - 1937	Arthur Hearne
1937 - 1948	Oliver James Barley
1948 - 1949	Frederick William White
1949 - 1950	Elizabeth White
1950 - 1959	Walter Henry Wood
1959 - 1960	John Haydon Beaupre Carter
1960 - 1964	Cyril James Keir
1964 - 1972	Mr C A Lee
1972 - 1975	William Arthur Hawthorn
	Ernest Ainsworth Jenkins
1975 - 1977	David Carrington Sizer
1977 - 1981	Ernest Glenn Bryson
	Frederick Alan Rose
1981 - 1982	Sharron Debra Loraine Jennings
	Frederick Alan Rose
1982 - 1984	Ernest Glenn Bryson
	Sharron Debra Loraine Jennings
	Frederick Alan Rose
1984 -	Wayne Lindsay Bonner

Anchor

1775 - 1789	Thomas Cripps
1791 - 1796	Martha Cripps
1802 - 1824	Thomas Davis
1830 - 1867	John Webster
1868 - 1869	Richard White
1871 -	Susannah White
1876 - 1877	James Lambourn
1881 -	William Brown
1882 - 1883	Benjamin Goss
1887 -	Henry Taylor

LICENSING (CONSOLIDATION) ACT 1910.

At the General Annual Licensing Meeting holden at the County Hall in Oxford on the Fifth Day of February, One Thousand Nine Hundred and Twenty-one, for the Division of Bullingdon in the County of Oxford.

THE LICENSING JUSTICES for the said Division, HEREBY GRANT unto Mark Wells —— of Thame —— in the County of Oxford, Beerhouse keeper, by way of renewal this Justices' License authorising him to hold an excise license to sell Beer and Cyder by retail at the Licensed Premises situated at Thame —— aforesaid, for consumption either on or off the premises.

The owner of the premises in respect of which this License is granted ~~are~~ is Charles Lester of High Street, Thame

This License will be in force from the Fifth day of April next until the Fifth day of April, One Thousand Nine Hundred and Twenty-two.

Witness our hands

George H. Pope

Majority of the Licensing Justices present at the General Annual Licensing Meeting above mentioned.

Beerhouse License.

Beerhouse license for the Greyhound in 1921 (not collected)

1888 -	J Andrews
1891 -	George Simmonds
1895 -	Henry W Burnham
1899 - 1907	Thomas E Blood
1908 -	Joseph Harrowell
1911 - 1921	Walter Martin
1921 -	License not taken up

Angel

1673	Oliver Calcott
1675 - 1688	John Calcott
1688 - 1702	Richard Luce
1703 - 1711	Leonard Walker
	Angel and Crown
1712 - 1739	Leonard Walker
1744 - 1752	Henry Page
1753 - 1758	William Page

Angel Beer-house

1841 - 1843	James Towersey
1846 -	James Bonner

Bird Cage

	The Cage
1529 -	James Roose
1603 -	Philip Bird
1655 -	Philip Cotton
	1690 Mathew Crewes
1690 -	Thomas Edwards
1724 -	Alice Horwood
1728 -	Mary Cotton
1753 - 1762	Mary Knapp
	Bird Cage
1782 - 1807	Edward Turner
1808 -	John Turner
1809 - 1812	Edward Turner
	Bird in the Cage
1821 - 1847	Mrs Ann Turner
1850 - 1860	John Horton
	Bird Cage
1861 -	Richard Cooke
1863 - 1867	Henry Hayward
1869 - 1891	Henry Watson Burnham
1893 -	John Henry Peel
1895 - 1903	Henry Summersby
1907 - 1917	Charles Blood
1917 - 1918	Mary Blood
1918 - 1919	Charles Blood
1919 - 1937	Sydney Herbert Gaunt
1937 - 1938	Clara Gaunt
1938 - 1946	Charles Arthur Clarke
1946 - 1952	Ernest Edward Charles Rollings
1952 - 1954	Harold Charles Biley
1954 - 1963	Charles Higgins
1969 - 1988	Neville Hallam Ellis
1988 - 1992	Raymond Leslie Batstone
	Barry Sinclair Murphy
1992 - 1997	Wendy Wade (Batstone)
1997 - 1998	Stephen Louis Mitfin
1998 - 1999	George Albert Murphy
	Gordon Pennell
1999 - 2000	Melaine Nicola Baskerville
	Allison Catherine Neave
2000 -	Paul Barry Campion
	Monica Jane Knight

Black Boy

1693 -	Richard Moseley

Black Horse Hotel

	Fleur de Lys
1620 -	Jerome Gregory
1715 - 1736	Mathew & John Crewes
1768 - 1780	John Carruthers
1781 - 1789	Richard White
1792 - 1808	Joseph Richmond
1809 - 1832	Sarah Richmond
	Black Horse Hotel
1838 -	unknown
1841 - 1876	James Barton
1877 - 1887	James Stephens
1888 -	H Arnold
1891 -	Mrs Amelia North
1895 - 1899	Arthur Alfred Laybourne
1903 -	Alfred Yates
1907 - 1924	William Dunk
1924 - 1925	Edith Ann Dunk
1925 - 1928	Frederick Dudley Gerald Taylor
1928 - 1930	Frank Pearce
1930 - 1932	Henry Brown
1932 - 1934	Louis Seaton Rick
1934 -	Ann Howard
1934 - 1936	Henry Armitage Sanders
1936 - 1937	Lillian Mary Sanders
1937 - 1938	Robert Gordon Burns
1938 - 1939	Arthur George Denmark
1939 - 1940	Charles Fox
1940 - 1941	William Winter
1941 - 1942	Kathleen Fox
1943 - 1954	Kathleen Fox-Brown
1954 - 1957	Fred Irvins
1957 - 1962	Nancy Daniels
1962 - 1963	John Douglas King
1965 - 1973	James Federick Addington

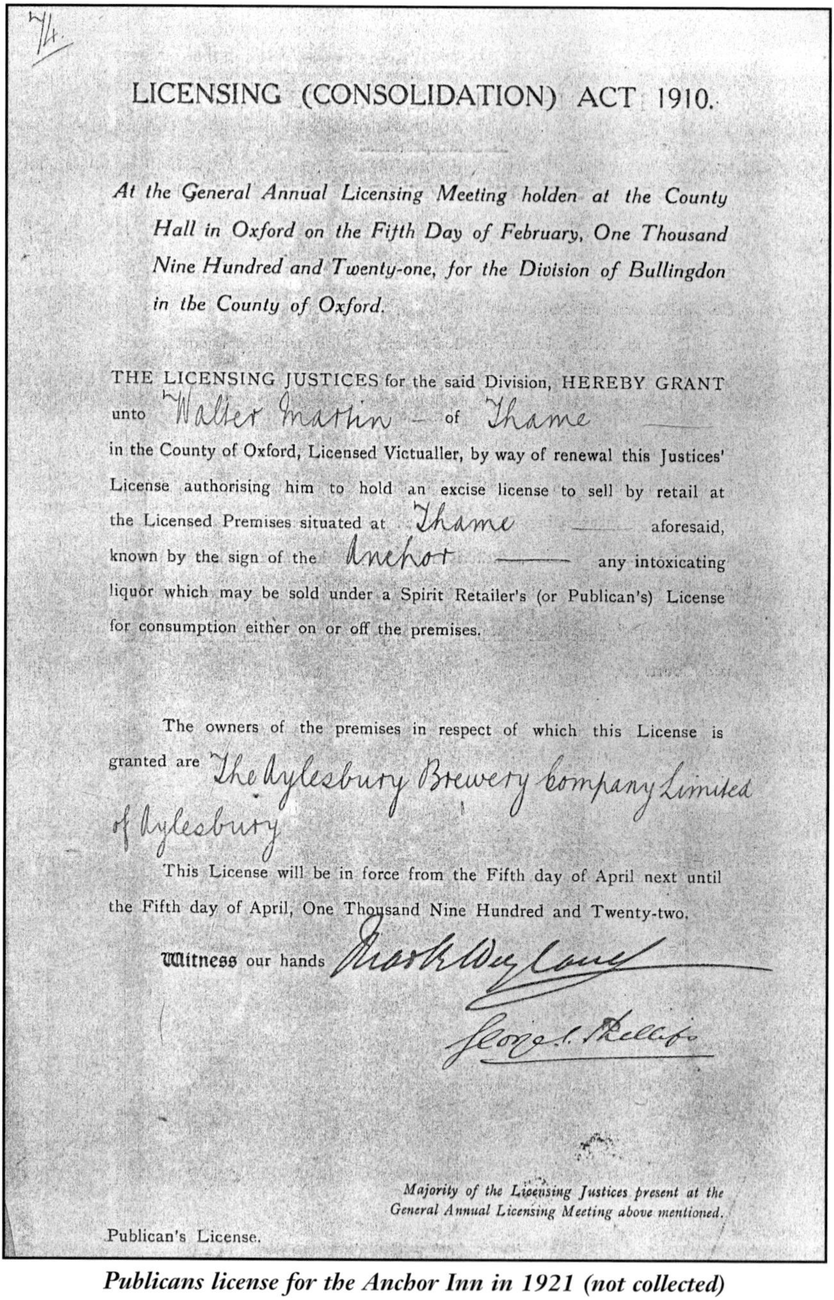

LICENSING (CONSOLIDATION) ACT 1910.

At the General Annual Licensing Meeting holden at the County Hall in Oxford on the Fifth Day of February, One Thousand Nine Hundred and Twenty-one, for the Division of Bullingdon in the County of Oxford.

THE LICENSING JUSTICES for the said Division, HEREBY GRANT unto Walter Martin — of Thame — in the County of Oxford, Licensed Victualler, by way of renewal this Justices' License authorising him to hold an excise license to sell by retail at the Licensed Premises situated at Thame — aforesaid, known by the sign of the Anchor — any intoxicating liquor which may be sold under a Spirit Retailer's (or Publican's) License for consumption either on or off the premises.

The owners of the premises in respect of which this License is granted are The Aylesbury Brewery Company Limited of Aylesbury

This License will be in force from the Fifth day of April next until the Fifth day of April, One Thousand Nine Hundred and Twenty-two.

Witness our hands

Majority of the Licensing Justices present at the General Annual Licensing Meeting above mentioned.

Publican's License.

Publicans license for the Anchor Inn in 1921 (not collected)

1973 - 1983	Patrick Jack Sanders
1983 - 1998	Peter Snow
1998 -	Adam Christopher Snow
	James Campbell
1998 -	Roy Weatherstone
	Maureen Janet Weatherstone
	Charles David Ansell

Black Lion

1699 -	William Adkins

Blue Man

1723	Richard Leaver
1753 - 1788	William Needs
1789 - 1796	William Needs Jnr
1802 - 1812	Elizabeth Needs
1821 - 1830	James Cooper
1841 - 1847	John Clisby
1850 - 1851	John Mead
1853 - 1854	Ann Mead
1861 - 1867	Alfred Seymour
1869 -	Francis Faulker
1871 -	Margaret Faulkner
1874 -	John Plater
1877 -	William George Howlett
1881 - 1883	Henry Pearce
1887 - 1891	George Price
1895 -	Walter Addison
1899 -	Henry Beard
1903 - 1906	George Glass
1906 -	De-licensed

Britannia

1838 - 1842	John Styles
1847 - 1851	Thomas Bonner
1852 - 1854	Biddy Bonner
1861 - 1864	Robert Hawes
1869 -	Mrs Harriet Hawes
1871 -	Charles Newitt
1874 -	Henry Green
1876 -	Henry Taylor
1877 -	William White
1881 - 1887	Susan White
1898 - 1904	James Southam
1907 -	George Seager
1908 -	Herbert Voller
1910 -	C Seager
1911 - 1912	James Pember
1912 - 1913	Edward Carter
1913	License renewal refused

Bull

1650	Stephen Cousin
1768 - 1780	Thomas Edden
1784 - 1787	Edmund Hall
1788 -	George Prickett
1789 - 1792	George Pilkington
1796 -	Mary Pilkington
1802 -	John Tucker
1804 - 1805	James Hester
1806 -	Thomas Holland
1807 - 1830	William Fowler
1841 - 1843	Edward Ledbeater
1846 -	David Plumb
1847 -	John Edden
1850 - 1854	William Webster
1861 - 1867	Thomas Wales
1868 - 1869	Thomas Seagrave Sutton
1871 -	Ephraim Wales
1874 - 1876	TC Sutton
1881 - 1882	Henry Woolhams
1883 - 1899	John Sutton
1903 - 1912	John Fowler
1912 - 1913	James Hedger
1913	License renewal refused

Bull Ale-house

1838 -	John Coles
1842 - 1847	William Webster

Chequer Ale-house

1753 - 1758	John Wall
1759 -	William Wheeler

Cock

1712	Humfrey Learner
1712 - 1751	John Ivery

Cross Keys

1841 -	Thomas Burnard
1847 - 1874	John Howlett
1876 -	Mrs Cannon
1877 -	Robert Wakelin
1881 -	Charles Dent
1882 - 1895	William Barefoot
1903 - 1920	Septimus Clare Gurney
1920 - 1925	Roland Tipple
1925 - 1937	Henry Tipple
1937 - 1956	Daisy Harriet Elizabeth Tipple
1956 - 1957	Ronald James West
1957 - 1963	Mabel Marion West

1971 - 1973	John Swanson
1973 - 1977	John Edward Woollard
1977 - 1980	Keith Sidney Bailey
1980 - 1982	Anthony Hammonds
1982 - 1994	Christopher Norman Whitmore
1994 - 1998	David John Whale
1997 -	Denise Ann Cousins

Crown Inn

1781 - 1792	Thomas Loveday
1796 - 1802	Henry Dimmock
1804 - 1805	William Simmons
1806 - 1812	William Croxford
1821 - 1823	Mary Simmons
1824 - 1830	John Simmons
1842 - 1846	William Phillips
1847 - 1854	Joseph Lester

Crown Beer-house

	Black Horse Ale-house
1837 -	Phillip Burnard
1841 - 1852	Thomas Steeden
	Crown
1861 - 1892	Joseph Lester
1895 - 1907	Thomas Grant
1907	De-licensed

Falcon

1861 - 1869	William Rush
1869 - 1874	Edward Webster
1876 -	John Greene
1881 - 1898	Thomas Dorsett
1899 -	Horace Young
1903 -	George Hart
1907 - 1920	Henry Taylor
1920 - 1939	Henry Cadwell
1939 - 1961	Maude Ethel Cadwell
1961 - 1963	Bernard Barefoot
1969 - 1972	Charles George Bish
1972 - 1982	Charles Edward Cole
1982 - 1987	Geoffrey Richard Williams
1987 - 1990	Constance Joan Rainbird
1990 - 1991	Michael Anthony Frith
1991 - 1992	Joan Mordue
1992 -	William McNeill
1992 - 1993	Stephen P Kerry
1993 - 1995	Helen Webb
1995 - 1996	Allan James Trowers
	Neal McPherson
1996 - 1997	Janet Gannon
1997 -	Barry Sinclair Murphy
	Wendy Batstone

Fighting Cocks

	Black Horse
1721-	George Bullen
	Fighting Cocks
1749 - 1755	Thomas Kent
1756 - 1757	Anne Kent
1757 - 1786	Thomas Kent
1788 - 1808	John Hurst
1808 - 1811	William Webster
1812 -	Josh Loveday
1821 - 1822	James Battin
1830 -	George Chapman
1842 - 1847	William Scadding
1850 - 1891	William Howlett
1895 -	Sophia Howlett
1899 - 1929	Alfred Howlett
1929 - 1962	Arthur James Howlett
1962 - 1963	Florence Emily Howlett

Four Horseshoes

1774 - 1796	Jonathan Bristow
1803 -	William Jemmett
1802 - 1806	Robert Howland
1807 - 1812	Robert Howlett
1821 - 1823	Robert Croton
1830 -	James Balls
1841 - 1846	Joseph Newitt
1847 - 1851	Joseph Newitt Jnr
1851 - 1852	George Newitt
1853 - 1854	George Francis
1861 - 1867	Thomas Newitt
1868 - 1871	John Fowler
1874 -	John Wheeler
1876 - 1891	John Young
1891 - 1926	John Thomas Young
1926 - 1948	Albert John Baverstock
1948 - 1960	Elsie Baverstock
1960 - 1962	John Maurice Dodwell
1970 - 1973	Edwin William Allsop
1973 - 1975	Thomas Bennett
1975 - 1982	Ronald Edward Hankin
1982 - 1987	Peter Whittaker
1987 - 1992	Donald John Cumming
1992 - 1993	Leigh Witney
1993 - 1994	Matthew Simon Thompson
1998	Licence not renewed

Fox

1848 - 1854	George Pywell
1861 - 1903	Richard Youens
1904 - 1906	Alfred Youens
1907 - 1912	Mrs Emily Youens

1912 - 1948	William Holland
1948 - 1951	Cyril George Stratford
1951 - 1952	Reginald Stanley Kempton
1952 - 1955	Herbert Thomas Line
1955 - 1958	Frank Thomas Leslie Fossey
1958 - 1959	William Henry Thomas Plasterer
1959 - 1962	Arthur Jesse Bowers
1962 - 1963	Dennis Sidney Tomkins
1971 - 1974	Henry Alexander Brandon
1974 - 1976	Derek Charles Goldsmith
1976 - 1984	David Barrie Flynn
1984 - 1987	Mavis Joan Flynn
1987 - 1990	Peter Snow
1990 - 1992	Tony Norman Tompkins
1992 -	Kyriacos Peros (Fish Shop)
1992	Licence not renewed

George

1769 - 1785	John Brown

Greyhound Beer-house

1841 - 1851	David Johnson
1871 - 1888	James Pollicott
1891 - 1898	Thomas Holland
1899 -	Elizabeth Holland
1903 -	Ann Holland
1911 -	Joseph Brown
1912 - 1915	Ralph Kilby
1915 - 1921	Mark Wells
1921	License not taken up

Greyhound Inn

1560	unknown
1617 - 1620	Peter Wilmott
1641 -	George Benson
1712 -	Thomas Baker
1712 -	John Cooke
1751 - 1759	Edward Stone
1760 - 1796	Richard Wall
1802 - 1823	William Wall
1830 - 1837	James Battin
1841 - 1843	Richard Linders

Half Moon

1868 - 1869	George Hawes
1871 -	John Lunn
1876 - 1883	Charles Newitt
1887 - 1919	James Soanes
1920 - 1923	Maria Soanes
1923	License not taken up

Hole in the Wall

	Eagle Tap
1851 - 1852	Mathias Hay
1861 -	Ann Philips
1870 -	Mrs Higgins
1871 - 1881	John Cope
	Hole in the Wall
1888 - 1889	William Howland
1891 -	William Chapman
1899 -	William Howlett
1903 - 1907	Edward Bartlett
1907	License refused

Jolly Sailor

	Sailor's Return
1853 - 1854	Ephraim Folly
1861 - 1864	Charles Howlett
	Jolly Sailor
1869 - 1883	Henry Arnott
1887 - 1895	William Wood
1899 - 1903	Charles Egleton
1911 -	Arthur Jackson
1911 - 1927	George Howland
1927 - 1937	George King
1937 - 1938	Albert Edward Taylor
1938 - 1945	Alfred George William Curtis
1945 - 1952	Walter Owen Lane
1952 - 1953	Jack Sidney Brown
1953 - 1963	Henry George Holmes
1971 - 1985	Jack Smith
	Wellington Hotel
1985 - 1992	Herbert Halliwell
1992 -	Bernard Hall
1992 - 1993	Stephen John Carr
1993 -	Paul Lohfink
1993 - 1994	William McNeill
1994 -	Licence not renewed

Nag's Head / King's Head

1560	unknown
1579 - 1681	John Robotham
1710 -	Mathias Crewes
1726 -	John White
1729 - 1750	John Fevin
1752 - 1758	James Bennett
1776 -	James Hope
1777 - 1780	Francis Moore
1781 - 1782	Thomas Rose
1783 - 1808	Robert Batting
1809 - 1861	Robert Battin
1863 - 1877	Mrs Ann Battin
1881 - 1923	Henry Robert Battin Arnold
1924 - 1935	Aubrey Charles Higgins

1936 - 1939	William Heath
1940 - 1945	Amelia Elizabeth Heath
1946 - 1959	Reginald Albon Gibson
1959 - 1963	Ronald Arthur Slate
1970 - 1978	Brian George Max
1979 - 1980	Michael John Talboys
1981 -	Alan James Jefferies
1982 - 1995	Gordon Lancaster
1996 -	Robert Frank Moore
	Mary Moore
1997 – 2000	Janet Freda Gannon

One Bell

1746 - 1748	Isaac Wheeler
1753 - 1755	Mary Wheeler
1778 - 1791	William Derrick
1792 - 1796	Sarah Derrick
1802 -	George Lambert
1804 - 1808	Rosetta Lambert
1809 - 1811	John Hurst
1812 - 1821	Thomas Hurst
1822 - 1824	Mary Hurst
1830 - 1858	Thomas Sheldon
1861 - 1869	George King
1871 -	John Wheeler
1874 - 1877	Elizabeth Holdaway
1881 - 1883	Henry Barney
1887 -	John Brewer
1888 -	Mrs A Turnham
1891 -	Thomas George Hounslow
1895 - 1898	John Goodenough
1899 -	William Preston
1903 -	William Spence
1907 -	William Kither
1908 -	Henry Burridge
1911 - 1914	Thomas Cast
1914	No licence application

Oxford Arms (High Street)

1753 - 1759	Robert Howland
1760 - 1761	Joseph Howland
1765 - 1770	Richard Gardiner
1784 - 1796	Richard White

Oxford Arms (Middle Row)

1841 -	Samuel Oliver
1842 - 1874	Richard Bowler
1876 -	Henry Newitt
1881 - 1882	Harry Bowler
1887 - 1888	Henry John Vickers
1891 -	Thomas Hester
1895 - 1898	Henry Baker
1899 - 1910	James Gibbs
1911 - 1937	Charles Robert Plumridge
1937 -	Elizabeth Plumridge
1937 - 1949	Harry Clarke
1949 - 1953	Arthur Henry William Parker
1953 - 1956	Noel Mulberry
1956 - 1957	Albert Edward Merriman
1957 - 1961	Winifred Mildred Merriman
1961 - 1963	Stanley Graham Pillinger
1970 - 1974	John Malcolm Viol
1974 - 1975	Michael Stewart Barraball
1975 - 1976	Roger Richardson
1976 - 1977	Leslie Frederick Knight
1977 - 1979	Eric Douglas Lewis
1979 - 1986	Donald Stoneham
1986 - 1990	Michael Christopher Dowling
	Arthur Roy Murray
1990 - 1991	Michael Christopher Dowling
1991 - 1994	Michael Ernest Davy
	Michael Christopher Dowling
	Hogshead
1994 - 1996	Brenda Blundell
1996 - 1997	Paul Barry Campion
1997 - 1998	Patrick White
	Market Square
1998 -	Anthony Julian Favell
	Nicholas William Corden

Plough

1841 - 1843	John Price
1844 - 1864	Hannah Price
1869 - 1882	James Pearce
1885 -	Mrs James Pearce
1887 - 1891	Thomas Blood
1899 - 1903	James William Blake
1907 -	Walter Bird
1908 - 1910	William Atkins
1911 - 1914	Horace Percy Chavasse
1914 - 1917	Joseph Parker
1917	Closed

Red Cow

1753 - 1784	Thomas Stevens
1785 - 1796	George Wheeler
1802 - 1822	William Bernard
1823 - 1830	John Bernard
1841 - 1868	Thomas Pearce
1869 - 1871	Arthur Wakelin
1874 - 1883	Thomas Boiling
1887 - 1907	Mrs Eliza Boiling
1907 -	Alfred Boiling
1909 -	Lewis Baldwin

1911 - 1914	John Plunkett
1914 - 1915	Alexander Brown
1915 - 1917	Edwin Hicks
1917	Licence withdrawn

Red Lion Inn

1530 -	unknown
1660 - 1688	Mr John Harris
1696 -	Thomas Heath
1710 -	Thomas Cannon
1726 – 1763	Thomas Smith
1764 – 1766	Richard Smith
1767 - 1787	Joseph Powell
1787 - 1789	Thomas Lovell
1789 - 1796	Joseph Powell
1802 - 1808	Robert Hawkins
1809 - 1816	Thomas Harris
1821 - 1824	Stephen Lovelock
1830 -	Alice Lovelock
1841 -	Mary Wyatt (Eating House)
1842 - 1843	Richard Hall
1846 - 1847	Richard Youens

Red Lion Beer-house

1863 - 1867	George Collins
1869 - 1874	Thomas Burnard
1876 -	Richard Burnard
1877 - 1881	William Burnard
1882 - 1888	Jabez Chapman
1891 -	Alfred Wm Read
1911 -	George Howland
1911 - 1915	John James Rawlings
1915	Closed

Rising Sun

1841 - 1847	William Webster
1850 - 1868	Thomas Webster
1871 - 1899	William Henry Webster
1903 - 1916	Charles Dover
1916 - 1918	William Ernest Dover
1918 - 1919	Charles Dover
1919 - 1929	William Ernest Dover
1929 - 1952	Ronald Hobbs
1952 - 1955	Thomas Lewes Gardner
1955 - 1956	John Roberts
1956 - 1974	Harold George Luckett
1974 - 1980	Gordon Sydney Churchill
1980 -	Anne Rosemary Scrivener
1980 - 1983	Alan Leslie Cogswell
	Pauline Mary Ann Cogswell
1983 - 1988	Lesley Susan Patience
	John Philip Patience
1988 - 1996	Robert David Edward Slater
	Marion Elizabeth Slater
1996 -	Michael Kenneth Constable
1996 - 1998	David Brown Simpson
	Joane Mary Simpson
1998 -	David Brown Simpson
	Nicholas Paul Humphries

Saracen's Head

1575	Nicholas Stanton
1575 - 1595	Richard Pitman
1617 -	Richard Pitman
1618 - 1624	Widow Pitman
1625 - 1633	Edmund Brookes
1634 - 1647	William Welsh
1656 -	Emmanuel Slaughter
1664 - 1668	Widow Slaughter
1669 - 1704	Richard Adkins
1729 - 1743	James Horseman
1744 - 1767	William Horseman
1767 - 1804	Christopher Wakelin
1805 - 1812	Robert Clisby
1821 - 1823	Elizabeth Clisby
1830 -	Sarah Clisby
1841 -	Elizabeth Edden
1842 - 1843	Edward Edden
1846 - 1874	Francis Seymour
1876 -	Daniel Seymour
1877 - 1899	Francis Seymour
1903 - 1912	John Adams
1912 - 1933	Thomas Kentish
1933 - 1948	Harry Cooper Lemming
1948 - 1950	John Stanley Voyce
1950 - 1951	Leon Dupont
1951 - 1963	James Joseph Harrison
1963	Records missing

Seven Stars

1774 - 1804	William Edden
1805 -	Thomas Holland
1806 - 1824	Francis Seymour
1830 -	Robert Seymour
1842 - 1847	James Ellson
1850 - 1854	Henry Pearce
1861 - 1867	Richard Pym
1869 - 1881	John Pearce
1883 -	William Lee
1886 -	Henry Pearce
1887 -	Joseph Corning
1888 -	T Baldwin
1891 -	Henry Williams
1898	Licence lost

Six Bells

1560	Unknown
1753 - 1766	Richard Gibbons
1767 - 1772	Grace Gibbons
1773 - 1785	Thomas Cope
1787 - 1830	Richard Gibbons
1841 - 1842	William Clisby
1844 -	James Batten
1846 - 1854	William Clisby
1861 - 1871	William Pearce
1874 - 1883	Emma Pearce
1885 - 1898	James Larner
1899 - 1903	George Cartland
1907 - 1913	Joseph Holland
1913 - 1922	George Robert Cartland
1922 - 1930	Richard Charles Taylor
1930 - 1933	George William Harpham
1933 - 1960	John William Howell
1960 - 1963	Albert Edward Jakeman
1966 - 1973	John William Gill James
1973 - 1975	Guy Chase
1975 - 1988	Philip John Stone
1988 - 1992	Philip John Hale
1992 - 1996	David Brown Simpson
1996 - 1997	Jonathan Andrew Greenwood
1997 - 1998	Sharron Ann Knight
1998 –	Richard Murray McDermid
	Angela Theresa McDermid

Spread Eagle Hotel

	Crown
1751 -	Richard Ewstace
	Spread Eagle
1837 - 1871	Charles Simmonds
1874 - 1899	William Liddington
1903 - 1921	Brighton Webster Liddington
1921 - 1922	Bertram Oswald Brewis
1922 - 1932	John Rowland Fothergill
1932 - 1936	Brighton Webster Liddington
1936 - 1937	William Thomas White
1937 - 1941	Brighton Webster Liddington
1941 -	Evelyn Dorothea Peaford
1941 - 1942	Ada Muriel Jessie Riordan
1942 - 1943	Thomas Alec Long
1943 - 1945	Joan Estcourt
1945 - 1949	Thomas Stewert Inglis
1949 - 1969	Claude Michael John Barrington
1969 -	David Maurice Lister Barrington

Star & Garter

1861 - 1877	James Timms
1881 - 1932	John Wells
1932 - 1933	Mary Charlotte Wells
1933 - 1951	Walter Mark Wells
1951 - 1953	Alice Maud Wells
1953 - 1960	Hubert Steel Brown
1960 - 1982	Cyril John Montague Boas
1982 - 1984	John Hammond
1984 - 1985	Doreen Kathleen Hammond
1985 - 1997	Elwyn Reginald Durrant
1997 -	Pamela Durrant

Swan

1595	Thomas Stribblehill
1595 -	Augustine Stribblehill
1756 - 1760	John Wyatt
1761 - 1762	Hannah Wyatt
1763 - 1764	John Bennett
1765 - 1779	Hannah Bennett
1780 - 1786	John Fowler
1787 - 1792	Henry Dimmock
1795 - 1798	John Fowler
1799 - 1812	John Fowler Jnr
1815 - 1825	Edmund Phillips
1830 - 1832	Hannah Phillips
1834 -	William Phillips
1841 - 1843	John Coles
1847 - 1867	George Phillips
1869 - 1888	Thomas Wales
1891 -	Edward Gibbs
1895 - 1912	George Albert Baker
1912 - 1923	John Adams
1923 - 1927	Ernest John Petty
1927 - 1928	Sydney Leslie Green
1928 - 1936	Thomas Watson Pearson
1936 - 1940	Frank Albert Merry
1940 - 1947	Henry Harold Parsons
1947 - 1957	James William Wainwright
1957 - 1959	Eileen Gertrude Wainwright
1959 - 1963	James Herman Beer
1963 -	William Charles Appleton
1985 - 1987	Tony Norman Tompkins
1987 - 1993	Sue Lynne McCoy Pridie
	David Philip Turnbull
1993 - 1994	Sue Lynne McCoy Pridie
1995 -	Sue Lynne McCoy Turnbull

Three Pidgeons

1753 - 1762	Elizabeth Dobbinson

Two Brewers

1832	unknown
1841 - 1854	Charles Bonner

1861 -	Priscilla Bonner
1863 - 1869	George Bonner
1871 -	Eber Hancock
1874 - 1877	Edwin Hicks
1881 - 1891	Charlotte Hicks
1895 - 1899	Edwin Hicks
1903 -	John Butler
1907 -	Edward Lawrence
1910 -	D Newman
1910 - 1911	George Edward Griffiths
1911 - 1914	William Frederick Waldram
1914 - 1915	Sylvanus George White
1915 -	William Seale
1915 - 1921	John Henry Turner
1921 -	Ann Turner
1921 - 1922	Percy Brandon
1922 - 1925	Alice Maud Brandon
1925 - 1927	Alice Maud Hill
1927 - 1954	Albert Henry Baker
1954 - 1958	George Harry Hall
1958 - 1960	Bessie Hall
1960 - 1964	Edward David Parker
1964 - 1972	Herbert William Preston
1973 - 1974	Elwyn Reginald Durrant
1974 - 1983	John Leslie George Bone
1983 - 1992	James Edward Thomas
1992 - 2000	Michael Ernest Davy

Wenman Arms

1869 - 1886	Thomas Newitt
1887 -	Percy Russell Tompkins
1891 -	Thomas Curtis
1895 -	William Harms
1898 - 1899	Walter Soanes
1903 -	Henry J Giddons
1907 - 1915	Charles Hawkes
1915 - 1923	Herbert Busby
1923 - 1930	Charles Hawkes
1930 - 1931	William Oliver Fawn
1931 - 1937	Herbert Isaacson
1937 - 1940	Aubrey Charles Higgins
1940 - 1947	Gertrude Bessie Higgins
1947 - 1954	Cabin Thomas Shirley
1954 -	Frank Driver
1954 - 1957	William James Moss
1957 -	Ceased to be licensed

Wheatsheaf

1850 - 1854	William Howland
1861 -	Richard Garner
1863 - 1864	Lawrence Webster
1869 - 1874	Mrs Lydia Webster
1876 - 1877	Herbert Lawrence
1881 - 1891	Richard Cornish
1891 -	Richard Hall
1895 - 1910	Thomas Sheppard
1911 - 1918	Frederick Young
1918 - 1954	Nellie Young
1954 - 1956	Henry William Harris
1956	Licence not taken up

Wheele

1623 -	Margaret Tomlinson
1656 -	Edward Tomlinson

White Horse

1784 - 1812	Robert Ewers
1821 -	Ann Ewers
1823 - 1830	Mary Ewers
1841 - 1852	Abel Hill
	William Latham
1853- 1867	Mary Ann Latham
1869 - 1895	John Seymour
1899 -	Eliza Seymour
1907 - 1908	Frank Seymour
1908	Temperance Hotel

Windmill

1749 – 1757	Richard Gibberd
1758 - 1786	Elizabeth Gibberd

Wood's Ale-house

1838 - 1853	Thomas Wood

Woolpack

1847 -	William Howlett
1850 - 1854	Thomas Burnard
1861 - 1863	Jesse Johnson
1964 -	Elizabeth Thrift
1871 -	Joseph Darvill
1874 - 1887	John Charles West
1891 - 1903	Robert Guntrip
1907	De-licensed

'I'm amused at the signs
As I pass through the town,
To see the odd mixture -
An Angel and Crown
The Sword and the Cock
The Bull and Greyhound
The Swan and Seven Stars
The Wheel and White Hound
The George and Red Cow
The Fox and the Falcon
The Plough and One Bell
The Sun and the Red Lion."

Adapted from British Apollo
- early 18th century periodical

Chapter Eight
Legislation and Social Development

In this delve into the history of the pubs of Thame, it is useful to know a little about how the English pub has developed throughout history, through the various phases of legislation, and through its social development. Not all of these developments will have necessarily affected Thame directly, but they do help to indicate the general trend leading towards the modern drinking establishment.

The reduction in numbers of pubs in more recent years has been in part due to the trading practices that resulted from Supply of Beer Order of 1989. This Act of Parliament, seen by many as the saviour of the small brewer, is only the latest in the long line of attempts by the Government to control and tax an Englishman's staple drink.

Henry II was the first to place a tax on ale in 1188, when his "*Saladin Tithe*" was imposed to raise money for the Crusades. Henry III in his *Assize of Bread and Ale* of 1267 is the earliest record of price fixing of ale. The price was set at 1d, 1½d and 2d per gallon dependant on strength.

The introduction of hops to English ale in the fifteenth century caused so much controversy that Henry VI had to proclaim "*that beer brewers be allowed to ply their trade*", despite the protests of the more traditional ale brewers. (To those readers perhaps unsure of the difference between medieval ale and beer; ale was a sweet dark brew generally enjoyed by Englishmen prior to the *adulteration* of the brew by the use of hops. The introduction of hops to the brewing process produced a lighter beer with a more bitter taste and a brew that remained palatable for longer).

Brewing had been around for a long while prior to Henry's Act of 1267. There is evidence that brewing of fermented Barley took place in ancient Egypt and the Middle East. So it is probable that brewing travelled to England at the same time that barley was introduced as a crop. By the time that the Romans introduced wine to Britain ale had become an established drink and they had great difficulty converting true Englishmen away from their tipple.

In these early times most brewing was carried out by monasteries, or at home by the women of the household. That which was not drunk by the family may have been sold in the local ale-house. The monasteries would have consumed much of their own brew but some would have been served in their hostels. Medieval pilgrims travelled around the country seeking their salvation at the numerous shrines and this led the monasteries and landowners to build dedicated hostels for the accommodation of the pilgrims.

Many of these monastic hostels were the forerunners of the inns we know today with the names such as Red Lion, Greyhound, Chequers, being derived from these times. Innkeepers would display the coat of arms of their landowner or landlord on a signboard outside their hostelry. The most prominent device on the coat of arms would often be taken by an illiterate populace to describe their favourite drinking establishment.

Barley provided the essential ingredient of the staple foods, bread and beer, and so when barley was in short supply the population would be likely to starve, unless action was taken to prevent it. In the dearth years of the sixteenth century parliament tried to control the use of barley and required all production to be recorded. The Corn Returns for Thame in 1587 give the names of 18 persons in New Thame and 3 in Old Thame who were brewing and baking. A typical entry is that of Richard Woodbridge: who; *dothe bake weakely 3 bushels and doth brewe 4 bushels and hath used it these 10 yeares.*

Although the King and parliament made the laws, it was left to the local authorities to enforce them. Consequently in these early years a method was needed to determine the quality and strength of the brew and therefore the price of the ale. These were the times before Original Gravity and the scientific apparatus with which to measure it. Towns would appoint local men as Ale Tasters to assess the quality of the brew and determine whether it was fit for drinking. The local market court in Thame appointed two Ale Tasters every quarter during the seventeenth century. Often these would be local victuallers, for instance William Tame and John Shepherd in 1649. Tradition says that Ale Tasters wore leather breeches and tested the quality of the ale by sitting for a while on a drop of liquid and seeing how sticky it became. The less sticky it had become the less sugar remained in the brew therefore the better the quality. Of course we do not know what the Ale Taster did with the rest of his quart (or do we).

Ale and later beer were the staple drink of all the population. The production process of mashing and boiling the liquor ensured that the water, which was previously undrinkable, was effectively sterilised and most germs and viruses killed. The first and therefore the strongest mashing was normally consumed by the men folk, women and children would drink the second and weaker mashing. This process of giving a second mashing of the wort gave rise to the term *small beer,* which in this case means weaker beer not *beer for small people.*

Price fixing and control of drinking have always seemed to be a part of life. Early in the seventeenth century, Oxfordshire magistrates issued their "**License to Keepe A Tipling House**". Most of these rules would not go amiss in pubs of today and neither would the price.

The seventeenth century saw many attempts to regulate drinking. In 1627 public flogging was authorised for drunks who did not pay their fines. In 1650 an Act was passed that forbade returning to an inn after midnight on a Saturday or leaving till 1am Monday. Taxes on beer were also on the increase, from two shillings and six pence per gallon in 1688 to three shillings in 1692. (Spirits at this time were taxed at tuppence per gallon.) The quality of the beer was also being controlled and in 1701 the use of anything other than hops as a bittering agent for beer or ale was forbidden. Most of these rules

License to Keepe a Tipling House

Oxon Memorandum We his Majesties Justices of the Peace undernamed have licensed Just: Egerly of Brittington husbandman to sell ale and beere and to use the trade of victualling within the said place for the space of one year next ensuing; And have taken Recognisance of him with two sufficient suerties according to the law and forme of the Statute in that case provided, not onely to observe and keepe the Articles heerunder written, but allso all other his Majesties Lawes and Statutes in theses cases provided.

In wittnes whereof we have heereunto sett our hand and seales the 22nd day of Aprill in the yeare of the raigne of our Soveraigne Lord James by the grace of god of England France and Ireland King defender of the faith etc.

Imprimis that he shall suffer no Neighbours Children or Servants of any other dwelling in the same parish to tipple in his house.

Item that none be suffered to tipple in his said house on the Sabbath or Festival dayes, at the sermon or service tyme, nor in any other day above one hower, nor at any tyme after 9 of the clocke at night.

Item that he suffer no Diceing, Carding, Playing at Tables or any other unlawfull game to be used in his house.

Item that he suffer no drunkerds, drunkeness, or any other evill rule to be in his house, if any happen to be, he shall presently acquaint the Constable, or other Officer with it, that such offenders may be punished, and such abuses reformed.

Item that if any vagabonds or any other suspitious persons come to his house and doe there offer any goods to be sold, he shall presently acquaint the Constable, or other Officer therewithall, that such persons may be apprehended and brought before some Justice of the Peace to be examined if there be cause.

Item that he brue his drinke, that he may sell the Best at 6s the barrell and the Small at 3s.

Item that he draw out his drinke and sell it by the Alequart and Alepint, and not by Cupps and Juggs, and sell the best for 3^{d} ye Alegallon, and the small at 2^{d} ye Alegallon.

Lawrence Tanfield, Gyles Bray

"License to Keepe a Tipling House" issued by Oxfordshire Justices 22 April 1617

and regulations were aimed at London and the other cities and it is generally agreed that few of them had any effect in the country towns and villages until the improvements in communications that were made in the mid 1700s.

In these days life was a great deal harder than in modern times and it cannot be disputed that many inhabitants drank far too much and took solace in their beer or ale. For many people life was just bearable through an alcohol induced haze. The introduction of tea and coffee in the seventeenth century offered a safe alternative to alcohol, but initially they were so expensive that *only the rich could afford to be sober.*

The majority of the ale-houses of the eighteenth century, were run by so called "ale wives" who would brew weekly for the market, opening their houses to visitors to the town in order to provide a meagre income for them and their family. Many of these establishments would only open on a market day and once that week's brew was sold it would be time to close and brew again for the following week.

Inns and ale-houses changed little until the social and civic reforms that were introduced during the Victorian era. Society then changed greatly and consumption of alcohol was seen by many as a sin in itself.

By the middle of the nineteenth century, drinking was considered by the government to be a serious problem across the country, especially the consumption of gin and spirits. To encourage the masses to turn to the lesser evil of beer, the Beer Act was passed in 1830. This Act abolished all tax on beer and permitted the sale of beer and cider by any householder who obtained a two-guinea license from the local Excise Office. This new freedom was seized upon by the brewers to encourage the opening of numerous small beer-houses, thus extensively opening up their own trade. Traditional inns continued to sell wines and spirits, their licences being granted by the local magistrates. There was however a £20 fine for beer sellers who sold wine or spirits. A large number of the current public houses in Thame originated as beer-houses, many only obtaining licences to serve wines and spirits in the 1960s.

Many politicians saw this radical act of 1830 as a step too far and gradually the freedom was reigned in. In 1848 licensed premises had to remain closed until noon on a Sunday and sales of alcohol to children under sixteen years old were banned.

1855 saw Sunday closing also enforced between 3pm and 5pm with final closing at 11pm. In 1869 the control of all licences was returned to the magistrates who were now under pressure to try to restrict the number of drinking establishments

The conditions in the Inns at this time was much different from what we expect today. Parsons tells it like this. *"it is true that in the good old days our for-runners did not bathe or wash very often, and the Thame water had a special reputation for foulness but they were not so particular as we are now and if the food and wine were good, did not mind sleeping two or three in a bed (I forget how many the Great Bed of Ware held) nor did fleas and other objectionable bedfellows trouble them overmuch. What did trouble them, however was that the innkepper was often in touch with thieves and highwaymen."* (The Great Bed of Ware is eleven feet and ten inches square and must have slept many people. It is now in the Victoria and Albert Museum.)

As a result of this the innkeeper was held responsible for any loss or damage to guest's property and so became very circumspect as to who he would admit, particularly late at night, as he may be subject to false claims against him. This caused a great deal of trouble for bona fide travellers and in 1863 the Innkeepers Act was passed. Inns that were registered under the Act were obliged to offer food and accommodation to any traveller, and his horse, at any time of day or night, but the inneeper was not liable for a claim of more than £30. Unfortaunately for those now wishing to claim this privilege the Act was repealed in 1921

The Licensing Act of 1904 gave magistrates the power to revoke licences and gave them instructions to reduce the number of drinking houses throughout the country.

From 1908 children under fourteen were forbidden from entering a bar. Then in 1910 greater powers were given to the magistrates to make the suppression of licences more effective and they were allowed to pay compensation for a lost licence. It is from 1910 that, in Oxfordshire, the records of the issuing of licences still survive.

The advent of the First World War saw the first general restriction of opening hours. Pubs were only allowed to serve from 6am to 9am and from 12.30pm to 10pm. Duty on beer was also affected by wartime measures and by 1918 had reached fifty shillings a barrel (36 gallons). Parliament restricted the sale of liquor to those over eighteen in 1923 but permitted the sale of non-spirituous liquor to sixteen year olds provided in was with a meal.

It is worth noting that most of these restrictions were introduced as temporary wartime measures but continued to be imposed until a beer loving Chancellor encouraged the relaxation of the opening hours in the 1990s.

The Ordinary in the eighteenth century - still served in the Swan in the 1930's

Location Map of

The location of all the inns and public houses which can be identified from available records are highlighted on this extract from the 1881 Ordnance Survey map. Note the large number of premises on the south side of the High Street, now today's Cornmarket.

the Inns of Thame

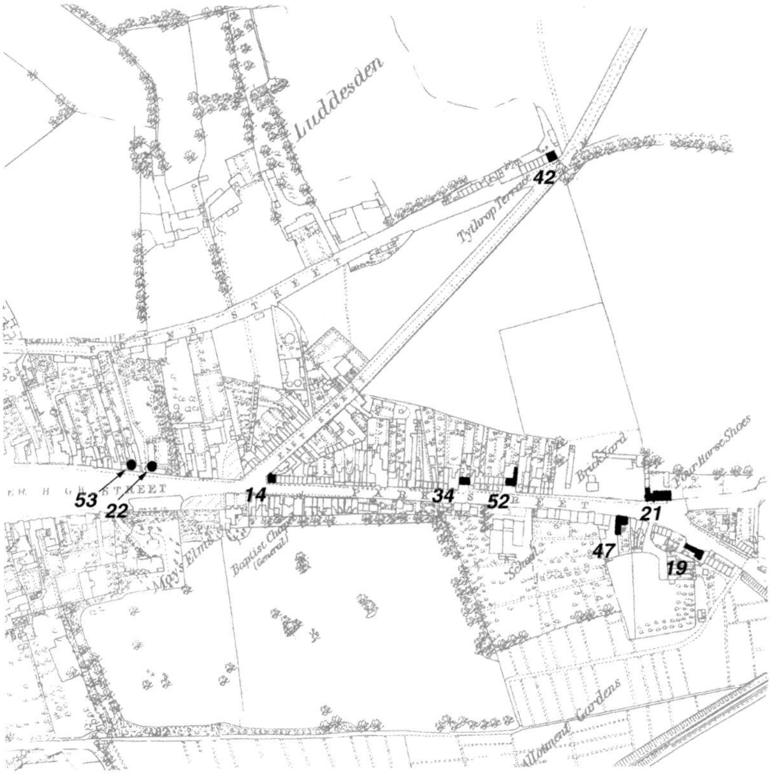

Individual names can be obtained from the references given in the index on page 84. Where certain pubs/inns cannot be accurately located, they have been identified with a ● indicating an approximate location.

Index to all the Pubs

Hogshead	124 Middle Row	31	40
Hole in the Wall	Southern Road	26	19
Jolly Sailor	54 Wellington Street	27	45
King of Prussia	Park Street	X	60
King's Ale-house	Upper High Street	28	32
King's Head	43 Upper High Street	29	13
Market Square	124 Middle Row	31	40
Nag's Head	43 Upper High Stree	29	13
One Bell	80 High Street	30	49
Oxford Arms	Cornmarket	41	16
Oxford Arms	124 Middle Row	31	40
Plough	Oxford Rd Priestend	32	56
Railway Hotel	Park Street	21	50
Red Cow	Aylesbury Rd	33	48
Red Lion Beer-house	33 Park Street	34	59
Red Lion Inn	1/2 High Street	35	21
Rising Sun	27 High Street	36	25
Sailor's Return	54 Wellington Street	27	45
Saracen's Head	Buttermarket	37	30
Seamon's Beershop	1 Upper High Street	38	43
Seven Stars	19 High Street	39	24
Six Bells	44 High Street	40	53
Spread Eagle Hotel	16/17 Cornmarket	41	16
Star and Garter	117 Wellington Street	42	57
Sun Inn	Sun Yard High Street	43	28
Swan	9 Upper High Street	44	32
Sword	High Street	X	24
Taplin's Inn	Lower High Street	45	56
Three Pigeons	High Street	X	33
Two Brewers	47 North Street	46	45
Wellington Hotel	54 Wellington Street	27	45
Wenman Arms	67 Park Street	47	60
Wheatsheaf	High Street	13	21
Wheatsheaf	57 North Street	48	43
Wheele	High Street	X	24
White Horse	12 Cornmarket	49	16
White Hound	Upper High Street	53	34
Windmill	High Street	50	21
Wood's Alehouse	44 Upper High Street	51	15
Woolpack	41 Park Street	52	59

Note: X indicates location unknown

We hope that you enjoyed Discovering the Inns of Thame as much as we enjoyed researching it. Although contrary to popular opinion only a small part was spent in the pubs themselves, most time was spent in various record offices. On count back, we have discovered nearly 80 different pub names in 61 separate locations. A book such as this can only relate what has gone before and it must be dependant on the people of Thame to ensure that the town maintains its tradition and that the 13 remaining pubs are kept for the people to enjoy.

Bibliography

The following sources have been widely consulted in the writing of this book:

Published Works

A History of Thame and its Hamlets, H. Lupton, 1860
A History of Thame, Brown & Guest, 1935
Beer and Skittles; Richard Boston 1976
Brewing and Breweries, Maurice Lovett, 1981
History and Antiquities of Thame Church, Rev. Dr. F G Lee, 1883
The Inns of Thame, Dr F G Parsons, Thame Gazette 1944
The Book of Thame, Gerald Clarke, 1978
The English Pub, 1994 Peter Haydon,
Victoria County History of Oxfordshire, Vol.6, 1962

Unpublished References

19th Century Trade Directories, Centre for Ox Studies,
Census Returns 1841 - 1881
Corn Returns for Oxfordshire 1586/7, SP12 198, Public Record Office
Courage Brewery Records, MS.dd.B5/40 – Oxon Arch
Court of Requests, 2/42/110
Earl of Abingdon property deeds,1622 – 1844, Bodleian Library
Giles Mompasson's "Account of the Fines and Profits for lycences of Innkeepers" 1617-20, Bucks Record Office
Halls Brewery Records, MS.dd.C.38 – Oxon Arch
Licensing Record Books, 1910 – 99, Oxon Magistrates Court (Thame & Henley Division)
Aylesbury Brewery Records Bucks Record Office,
Oxfordshire Quarter Session Rolls, 1687 – 1783, OxArch
Poor Rate Valuation List, 1882 – 6, Oxon Arch
Private Deposits (Property Deeds etc.). 17th – 20th C, Oxon Arch
Register of Electors, 1837/8, Oxon Arch
Thame Church-wardens Accounts, 1634 – 1801
Thame School Accounts, 1575 – 1814
17th – 18th cent. wills and probate documents
Victuallers Recognizances 1753 – 1822, OxonArch

"The Abbot of Burton brewed good ale,
On Fridays when they fasted -
But the Abbot of Burton ne'er tasted his own
As long as his neighbours' lasted."

(Old Ballad)